Presented To:

From:

Date:

Contending for Rest

Contending
For
Rest

Paul Y.S. Koo

ISBN: 9781696220903
9781999281908

Endorsements

Thank you, Paul, for writing such a timely needed book. I believe that there are many literally dying for the revelation found in these pages. This book has impacted me to be more diligent in the vital work of entering His Rest. I believe your life will prosper in every way as you contend for rest.

- **John Burns**, *Founder,*
Relate Church & ARC Canada.

In the Christian walk, discovering how to contend for rest is extremely crucial especially as we navigate through the inevitable storms of life, the earthquakes of emotional traumas and personal setbacks, or other shock waves of life that can cause us to crumble. Furthermore, to achieve our full God given potential or succeed in any avenue of life – knowing how to contend for rest and walk in it day in and day out is key to living out a fruitful Christian life.

Pastor Paul Koo in this powerful book "Contending for Rest" has introduced us to Biblical truths and insight on how we can contend for rest—and rest our way to success. Along with this, Pastor Paul has presented a powerful insight to ignite the fire of a soul, to enrich the depth of a spirit, and to encourage even the most discouraged person. A vital, vibrant, and victorious life can be discovered, developed, and displayed as a person incorporates these powerful insights from the Written and Living Word of God into everyday life.

In reading this amazing book and learning about "Rest" my life has been impacted and empowered to contend for rest and to rest my way to success as I serve in the Kingdom of God. Every chapter of this book has taught a powerful principle of Biblical insight about Rest and its Importance. I must candidly say that this book is a true life-changing and life-inspirational book that I strongly recommend to everyone.

- **Dr. Kazumba Charles**, *Founder/President Kingdom Insight TV Network*

We often think that to rest is easy, we just do nothing. However, in his book "Contending For Rest" the author shares his own journey of learning how to not depend on his own resources or looking for the next big thing, but rather to trust God. It is moving from the bondage of fear into the walk of faith, in order to enter the rest of God. It is doing the work of trusting God, often in the midst of difficulties that requires the most spiritual discipline and focus. Paul invites us to examine our own journey to find rest in God's Presence.

- **Steve Fleming**, *Founding and Senior Pastor, Koinonia Christian Fellowship*

Pastor Paul Koo brings practical and scriptural insight into one of the most pressing issues of our time. In a chaotic and rapidly changing world filled with deadlines, pressures to perform and compete in comparison to others, how do we reconcile the Lord's promise of Rest with these ever-increasing demands on us?

This book provides a clear path to find that Rest based on eternal biblical principles and presents a challenging self-analysis, again scripture-based, to enable the motivated reader to begin the journey to the place of tranquillity from which we can function effectively and successfully in the centre of God's plan and purpose for our lives.

Paul is to be commended for the personal transparency displayed here as he recounts his own journey in discovering and embracing this principle. He speaks with a Pastor's heart and a Prophet's boldness encouraging the reader to distinguish between the urgent and the important on the pathway to Rest.

- **Bishop Gordon McDonald,** *General Superintendent Pentecostal Holiness Church of Canada*

As a media producer, Paul Koo's book is a must read. "Contending for Rest" is a definite go-to-guide. In a fast-paced world, I've noticed a difference in my personal and work life as I've applied the Biblical principles outlined in this book. Paul's own experience has turned into a brilliant piece of work!

-Robert Melnichuk, *Director Western Canada,YES TV*

In this very competitive and performance-based culture we live in, you might be surprised to learn a rarely understood revelation that will truly give you an edge. Most are convinced that the only way to success and living well is to work harder, "by the sweat of our brow!" But instead of expansion, we end up with exhaustion. In this book, my friend Paul Koo shares his personal journey of "success" through a seemingly very unconventional way: REST.

Here you'll discover amazing principles based on fresh scriptural insights of REST that will help eliminate stress and bring peace to your soul, health to your body, and supernatural sustainable success!

- **Dr. Phil Munsey,** *Chairman*
Champions Network of Churches with Joel
Osteen/Lakewood Church

Pastor Paul Koo has served on the board of our ministry in Canada for 7 years. During that time, we have seen his passion for people and for God. *Contending for Rest* continues to demonstrate both. The simple and central message of this book, rest, is a word for today. When we can truly rest in just how much God loves us, I believe He will take us places we've never even dreamed!

– **Joel Osteen,** *Senior Pastor*
Lakewood Church

DEDICATION

To my fellow sojourners of life who are struggling every day to great exhaustion. My prayer is that you will find true rest and escape the vicious cycle that has caught so many of us and "enslaved" us to the system of the world in perpetuity.

"It is for freedom that Christ has set us free…"
Galatians 5:1 (NIV)

ACKNOWLEDGMENTS

I thank God for the many who have travelled with me on this
journey of rest. The longest, most patient and enduring
partner of this journey is none other than my most precious
wife, Wanna. I also want to thank God for my children who
in their own way had also taught me how to rest. Finally, I
want to thank the many dear and faithful brothers and sisters
in my church (Willowdale) who had been on this journey with
me. Thank you for "sticking around" and faithfully serve
God and support me. Especially in times when things were
uncertain and you did not even agree with everything that I
did and said. I love you all.

Foreword

I can't sit down; there's just too much to do.
If I don't handle it, who will?
Time for a vacation? Please. If I stop, I'll never get ahead.

Four-five hours of sleep a night is all I really need.
I can't let the competition catch up. I must stay two steps ahead
in order to succeed.

I'm doing God's work; of course, I can't slow down.

Man, I sure am tired.

In our fast-paced, driven, success-oriented, money-hungry, one-upmanship society, you've probably said or thought at least one of the above phrases in the past year, maybe even in the past week. You've learned from school that the "A" students get all the pats on the back, the fancy stoles at graduation, acceptance into prestigious universities, and much-needed scholarship money. On the job, you've experienced pressure to produce, the tension of meeting deadlines, and constant competition for raises and promotions. Then comes Sunday and the frenetic pace and continual demands do not stop. The expectations at church apply the same amount of stress that the world applies. Raise more money, increase the congregation, preach more exciting sermons, conduct more seminars, attend more conferences, perform more baptisms, construct bigger buildings.

Didn't Jesus invite us to come to Him and He'd give us rest? Why are we not at rest? Why are we so drained, weary, jaded, dissatisfied… and disobedient? Pastor Paul Koo has learned the secret of true, Biblical rest. *Just Rest* gently ushers us into the place of rest where God wants us. Kick back with this book in hand long enough to:

- Take a glimpse into your current reality of life's hustle and bustle
- See how God's own people, the children of Israel, jeopardized their rest
- Understand why we feel the need to go, go, go
- Learn how to pull rest into your reality
- Open your understanding to much more about true, Biblical rest.

You will come away from this book with your shoulders relaxed and the new lifestyle of rest down in your spirit. Jesus truly will have given you rest.

Rev. Dr. Sharon Norris Elliott
Editor, Author, Rest seeker

CONTENTS

Contending for Rest

Chapter 1

How It All Started

Several years after I started the current church that I am pastoring, I found myself facing a very unpleasant situation: There was no growth in my small congregation. Our leadership team had tried every technique and method that I had learned from attending different church growth seminars and conferences. We fasted, had overnight prayer meetings, organized worship and gospel concerts, hosted different spiritual conferences, staged community carnivals, trekked door-to-door, and participated in other evangelistic outreaches. I travelled to

1

the ends of the earth searching for that "holy grail" of church growth. I thought maybe the answer could be found in different countries where large churches were thriving like Columbia, South Korea, Singapore, and various places in the U.S. After all of these efforts to grow my church, the congregation still topped out at only about 50 people. Although we may have an increase in attendance whenever we invited a well-known speaker or musician, as soon as the "show" was over, the Faithful 50 would be the only ones still there.

In the meantime, I heard various news of breakout in different churches all over the world. You can imagine how frustrated I was.

One day, I decided to embark upon a 21-day fast to concentrate specifically on this church growth issue. At the end of my endeavor, I expected that heaven would open right before me, Jesus would walk into the room and tell me what I needed to do, revival would hit, major growth would take place, and I would see all my dreams come true. Alas, at the end of that fast, there was not even a peep from heaven. Nothing. Nada! Naturally, I came to the end of myself. I concluded that nothing was ever going to happen. So, I started to make arrangements to quit full-time ministry all together. I did not want to "waste" the prime of my life on chasing this empty dream of pastoring a church full of excited congregants, all growing in the Lord, and changing the community around us.

As I was about to quit ministry (I had received an offer to go back to work for a high-tech company), two things happened. First, the Lord moved upon a respected denominational leader to call out of nowhere and ask to see me. He told me he was in town to take care of some business for his denomination (which I wasn't part of), but the Holy Spirit told him to clear his schedule and come to meet with me. He had a specific instruction from the Lord to tell me. This dear friend of mine is an older gentleman and is a well-respected and well-known spiritual leader in our nation. When we sat down for breakfast later that morning, he told me that he knew I was going to go back to my old secular vocation and that he was sent by the

Lord to tell me not to do so. Needless to say, I was very stunned and glad at the same time. I was stunned because the God of the universe actually cared about what I was doing and He had sent His servant to speak to me. I was glad because I now knew for sure that my life in ministry was not of my own imagination, but was truly the plan of God.

The second thing that happened took place when I went to the Lord later in prayer. I heard a still small voice in my heart. It was like a thought. I later learned that this was how God speaks to me. The voice said, "Stand down!"

I thought to myself, *Stand down? What does that mean?*

As I continued to wait before the Lord, the instruction became clearer. I felt in my heart the message to "stand down" meant that for a season I was to do absolutely nothing! That idea was completely counterintuitive to me. You see, in all my years of working in a secular job, I functioned as either a sales executive, a sales manager, or a vice president of sales. Those jobs required that I do everything in my power to make the quotas. I would leave no stone unturned until I met my goals. That's how I was taught to be successful.

But now, I clearly understood that God was telling me to do something totally opposite to all I had ever practiced. So, being obedient to what I believed was the voice of God, I started to shut down all the activities in the church, from small groups to the various services we held. I contacted all the guest speakers and musicians that I had arranged for the various conferences that we would have annually and I told them that I was cancelling everything. The only formal activity that we maintained was the Sunday service. We did not have a guest speaker for the next 7-8 years.

I also made the decision that I was going to personally "stand down" and do absolutely nothing except focus on prayer and the Word. I found myself spending lots of time doing nothing in ministry except preaching and loving people. I also spent lots of time with my family and at home. Every time thoughts of church attendance or finances would enter my mind, I would reject them. I said to the Lord that if He wanted to shut this church down, I was okay with it. If He was going to build His church, He would have to do it on His own, and all I was committed to do was rest, pray, study His word, learn to hear His voice, and obey His instructions.

I reasoned with myself that if building this church was not the Lord's idea, the ship was going to go down quickly; therefore, its sinking would be a sign for me to abandon this whole ministry idea. But, if it was of the Lord for the church to survive, God would see to it that we would see growth and have enough funds to operate. Either way, I was resigned not to worry about church or ministry. In fact, I told a few friends in ministry that I had retired!

Within the next year or so, after I "retired" to rest in the Lord, the church started to grow all by itself. Strangers began to show up with no invitation from me nor from any effort we put in. People started to get healed during our Sunday services and our finances started increasing. Around that time, we had over 200 kids attending our Summer Camp. All of this was an amazing sight to witness.

Since then, we have seen the church grow to the point that by the time this book was being written, we have had to start scheduling a second service, and we sometimes run out of parking spaces. And even though we are now busier and have more ministries and staff, we endeavor to stay in and operate from that place of rest. From time to time, we see attendance and finances decrease for reasons that were beyond our control, we would resist the temptation to worry and get out of our commitment to rest and surrender.

On this journey, we have learned that when we operated from a place of rest, we could hear better from the Lord, started living healthier and longer lives, enjoyed life more, and became more effective in all that we did. I want to invite you to embark on this journey that will get you into that place of rest. Why? Because life is sweeter when you are at rest, you will see God do more miracles when you are at rest, and life is too short to waste it away in stress and sorrow.

Chapter 2

Current Reality

In the modern economy we are living in, people are always looking for solutions to relieve their stress. They know that stress contributes to many health problems we have today: heart disease, diabetes, cancer, miscarriage, just to name a few. In a recent study done in the United States[1], it was discovered that 77% of the people surveyed experience physical symptoms caused by stress. A full 73% of them regularly experience psychological symptoms

---

[1] Source: American Psychological Association, American Institute of Stress, NY, Research Date: 7.8.2014

caused by stress, 48% felt their stress level had increased over the past 5 years, and 33% of them felt they were living with extreme stress.

God in His goodness and grace has provided humanity the best stress relief solution: Rest. The Bible is actually a manual for rest. Jesus' calling of humanity is actually a calling to rest[2]. The promise of our faith is actually a promise to come into the perfect state of rest[3]. So why are so many believers not in rest? What is the disconnect?

I would submit to you that believers today, by in large, are as stressful if not more stressful than their unbelieving counterparts. Not only are Christians just as stressed as non-Christians in trying to survive, but Christians are more stressed when they come into the church. They are stressed about trying to live a perfect life. They are stressed about their own struggles with sin. They are stressed trying to live up to the expectations of others,

---

[2] Matthew 11:28-29
[3] Hebrews 4:3

and they therefore feel stress over whether or not they are living up to God's expectations.

In this book, I'd like to show you how to obtain perfect rest, a rest that is so true and rich that living in it will allow you to experience greater joy, greater fulfillment, and greater peace. Even when the world around you seems to be falling apart, you will find yourself in that perfect rest. What I want to show you is rest in perpetuity. In other words, you will be living in a constant state of rest, not just when you are on vacation or having a quiet retreat, but even in the busiest and most chaotic situation, you will find yourself in that state of rest. I pray that by the time you are finished with this book, you will have discovered and entered into the promised rest your Heavenly Father has prepared for you.

Biblical Rest

Before I tell you how you can get into that perfect state of rest, which is a Biblical rest, I want you to understand the concept of rest in the eyes of God. Many people think that when Jesus said rest, He meant for them to lie down in bed or in some hammock and do nothing. Though, rest may include lying down and doing nothing for a season, that type of physical rest is not the actual rest the Bible promises. Let's take a look at what the Bible says about rest. Hebrews 4:1-11 states:

> *"Therefore, while the promise of entering his rest still stands, let us fear lest any of you should seem to have failed to reach it (the rest). For good news came to us just as to them (the Jews in Moses' days), but the message they heard did not benefit them, because they were not united by faith with those who listened... For he has somewhere spoken of the seventh day in this way:* **_"And God rested on the seventh day from all his works."_** *... for whoever has entered God's rest has also rested from his works* **_as God did from his._**

> *Let us therefore* **_strive to enter that rest,_** *so that no one may fall by the same sort of disobedience"* (ESV, parenthetical notes and emphasis added).

Here we read that God rested from his own works. From that, people would assume that God stopped doing any work after He created Adam and Eve. Yet in John 5:17, thousands of years after the creation of mankind, Jesus said that "my Father (God) is (still) working until now as I am working." In other words, from the time the Bible declared that God rested from His own works to the time when Jesus was on Earth, God has been continually working. So, it would seem that the Bible is actually contradicting itself! This is only true if true Biblical rest actually means doing nothing! Rather, the human idea of rest is quite different from what God has in mind. Friends, you will learn that the true spiritual is NOT doing nothing. The next question then is, what does true rest look like from the Biblical/eternal/spiritual perspective?

True Purpose of Exodus

According to Hebrews 4, the reason God took the Jews out of Egypt was so that they could rest. Yes, He wanted to fulfill His promises to Abraham. Yes, He wanted them to enter into the place of great abundance. But mostly, He had wanted to give the people of Israel rest: rest from the slavery of their Egyptian taskmasters, rest from being abused, rest from being bullied, and most importantly, rest in His presence.

Today, God continues to call His people out of the yoke of slavery, which is a place of great anxiety. Just as He had wanted to rescue the Jews from strife, stress, labor, and heavy burdens, God is calling many of us who are under tremendous burdens and yokes of the worldly system, to enter into His rest.

You see, like those precious Israelites in the days of Egypt, many of us are living under the same conditions. By the time we get home from a full day of work, we are completely exhausted. While we may not have taskmasters whipping us all the time, we are still under tremendous stress and fear to meet expectations. Our circumstances are often as harsh as those the Israelites faced in the days of Egypt. Like the Israelites, we are slaving away, not knowing when we will be able to really live in rest.

Furthermore, today many believe that they are free but in reality, they are not free at all. They say they are free from sin, yet they are still struggling with sins. They say they are free from the worldly system, yet they are still under all kinds of yokes: mortgages, debts, multiple financial obligations, workplace stresses, and domestic problems. So they have to keep braving through to the point of complete exhaustion. This is not freedom.

Friends, do you know that it is God's desire to get you out of that place of exhaustion, slavery, and heavy yokes, so that you can enter into His promised rest? Do you know that it is His desire that even if there are storms, hardships, or challenges around you, you can still experience absolute rest? You may have bosses who don't like you, colleagues who hate you, children at home who are not listening to you, or some unexpected expenditures coming upon you, but God's promised rest can be near and present. Even as Jesus slept in the storm[4], God wants to give us that same supernatural rest through all our troubles and struggles.

---

[4] Mark 5:35-41

Chapter 3

In Context

Before we go any further, I want to address the context of Hebrews 4:1-11 which was mentioned in the previous chapter. The reason I want to do that is to make sure that we understand further what rest is NOT (again, from the Biblical/spiritual/eternal perspective.)

Readers need to realize that the author of Hebrews was trying to address some issues that were causing a great confusion and a division in the church. Specifically, in Hebrews chapter 4, the writer is addressing the false doctrines of salvation that were prevalent in the first century church. The false doctrines stated that salvation and righteousness cannot be gained through Christ alone, but one must also observe the Hebraic Law and traditions (circumcision, Sabbath, etc.)

Yes, false teachers of the early church would often be found going into various Christian gatherings and spreading these erroneous doctrines, telling people that faith in Christ alone was not enough. In order for people to be truly righteous and sanctified, and therefore fully accepted by God, they would also need to add their own works. These bogus teachers taught that unless people fully worked out their sanctification, they would not be qualified to be called a child of God, and thus would not be qualified to receive His blessings such as healings and provision. They would say, while you may be "saved," you are not really righteous, and therefore you are not qualified to receive God's blessings and mercy until you work out your own sanctification.

These false teachers put the burden of sanctification and being righteous squarely on the shoulders of individual believers. Believers not only need to have faith in God, they would say, but they also need to observe the Law, rules, and traditions, which were often manmade. In Galatians 2:4, the Apostle Paul called these false teachers of the law "false brothers" who had come into the Christian gatherings to spy out the freedom of the believers.

What freedom was Paul talking about? Paul was talking about freedom from the works of the Law, and freedom from the many requirements laid upon believers to be "right with God." Ultimately, the freedom to which Paul was referring is from sin and sin's condemnation. This is the freedom that is true rest in God.

Resisting Religious Burden

Galatians 5:1 states that it was "for freedom Christ has set us free," and we are to "stand firm therefore and do not submit again to a yoke of slavery." In other words, reject those ideas that say, "In order to experience God's rest, you must put up with all kinds of religious bondages." Apostle Paul tells us that we must stand firm. Stand firm in your freedom. Don't let anybody steal your freedom from you. Stand firm in the freedom you have found in Christ; freedom from condemnation and freedom from religious guilt.

Wrong Ideas of Earning God's Love

We also need to remove two more erroneous ideas: the wrong ideas about striving for God's approval, and the wrong mindset about how we ought to live under His grace. So many sincere Christians today are living like those in other religions: working super hard to please God, and hoping that they'd do enough to earn His grace, approval, protection, and blessings. How I wish they would just see the truth and change their mindset about the God we serve. Friends, the God we serve is not like any other god in the world. Our God is the God of grace and mercy. He is a God who loves us so much that there is no more love to give. There is nothing we can do to earn an extra ounce of love from Him, for He has already poured out and exhausted His grace and love for all humanity for all time, forever!

In First Timothy 6:12, Paul is teaching Timothy, his young protégé, that he needs to fight the good fight of faith. Faith in what? Faith in the Gospel of Christ, the gospel of grace and mercy. The gospel that is outside human strife to attain God's favor and approval. You see faith in the accomplished works of Christ must be present in order for you to rest. You can't rest with no faith. A lot of people don't have faith in the grace of God or the bigness of the grace of God, so they keep striving for God's approval while feeling guilty and condemned all the time. Friends, if you're fully convinced that God has forgiven all your sin and that your standing before God never changes, you will find yourself in rest.

So, rest is never about practicing religious rules and rituals so that one can earn some favor from God, and ultimately rest. What then is rest? What does it look like?

Chapter 4

The Israelites Freedom

(True Biblical Rest Defined)

We had mentioned earlier that the main reason why
God had wanted the people of Israel to be free from the
Egyptians was so they could enter into His rest. He did not set
them free from one yoke of slavery to then have them enslaved
again to another system, people, or kingdom. He had
something in mind that would guarantee their freedom and rest
forever. What was it? We can find the answers if we pay
attention to what God wanted Moses to say to the Pharaoh of
Egypt regarding the Jews. There are three things Moses was
instructed by God to tell Pharaoh regarding the Israelites
leaving Egypt.

Rest Through Feasting

First, God told Moses to tell Pharaoh that the people of Israel were to go into the wilderness to have a feast before the Lord.[5] In other words, what God had in mind about rest for the people of Israel was to have a feast! To truly rest before Him is to able to have a feast before Him. Not only were the Jews to have feasts in the Wilderness, but as we read on in the Old Testament, we see that the Israelites were to feast often before the Lord, even after they had possessed the Promised Land. In fact, there were seven feasts that the Jews were to celebrate every year without ceasing! Feasting was as important as observing all the laws and commands of the Lord. Why? Because feasting was rest for them!

Do you know what it means to have a feast? I'm not talking about just any party. I'm talking about a Biblical feast before the Lord. In the Bible, the feasts were always elaborate with lots of sacrifices (by the hundreds of thousands of animals at time[6]), and lots of eating and drinking before the Lord. Contrary to what you may have been told, our God is a God of

---

[5] Exodus 5:1

[6] 2 Chronicles 7:5

feasts! He loves to party. He enjoys seeing His people enjoying themselves in His presence.

For example, there was one time, hundreds of years after the Israelites left Egypt, when the Word of the Lord was being read before the people, the people were deeply touched and they wept. But Nehemiah (Governor of Jerusalem) and Ezra (the priest) reminded the congregation that "this day is holy to the Lord your God. Do not mourn or weep." Nehemiah further said, "Go and enjoy choice food and sweet drinks, and send some to those who have nothing prepared. This day is holy to our Lord. Do not grieve, for the joy of the Lord is your strength."[7] It is as if Nehemiah and Ezra were saying to the people, "Come on, let's party. Let's have a great feast. Because as we do, the joy of the Lord will come to us. We'll be refreshed and rested in our spirit."

One of the most powerful Biblical forms of rest is feasting: celebrating and enjoying ourselves in the presence of the Lord with His people. This rest restores our strength and renews our hope. If you are an individual who has never been part of a church that truly celebrates before the Lord when they

---

[7] Nehemiah 8:9-10

come together, it's time to look for a church where the people of God are celebrating God's goodness all the time. I often say to my congregation that our church should be like a hospital: a place that heals, restores, and renews those who come in. One of the most powerful and Biblical ways to renew people's strength, hope, and joy is feasting and celebrating before the Lord.

Every Sunday at Willowdale, we do our best to celebrate or encourage people to celebrate before the Lord through their praise and worship. In addition, every year at Willowdale, we also have three to four feasting (food) events. People bring food to the church for Thanksgiving, Easter, and Christmas, but also for whatever reason we can find to party (feast.)

Coming to church should consist of more than just singing a few songs and listening to some guy talking. I believe the heart of the Father is crying out and saying, "I want my people to get out of the yoke of slavery. I want My Christians to come away from the world (Egypt) and feast, party, and rejoice before Me. I want them to have a good time before Me. That's how they can find true rest in Me."

Rest Through Serving

God said to Moses, "I want you to tell Pharaoh that I want My people to leave your bondage and your system of oppression, so that they can come out to the wilderness." To do what? To serve Him.[8] Do you know that serving God is another supernatural and Biblical way to rest? I know it sounds very counterintuitive. One would think resting means to cease from work. After all, even God rested from all His works[9]. Yet, as I mentioned earlier, Jesus seemed to say quite the contrary. In John 5:17, Jesus said that since the creation of mankind, "My Father has been working until now, and I have been working."

You see, therein lies the secret of supernatural rest that most people have not experienced because it's so counterintuitive. Serving the Father in worship or in service to others is tremendously refreshing. Many people seem to have the idea that when they go to church on the weekend, they can just kick back and have someone serve them. Their mindset is that those who serve are *their* servants, and that their offerings (if they give at all) entitle them to be served. Yet Jesus said that

---

[8] Exodus 4:22; 7:16; 8:1,20; 9:13; 10:3
[9] Genesis 2:2

even He Himself did not come to be served, but to serve[10].
Now there are some who are too wounded or are in too much
pain to serve. Perhaps they are in a season in which they should
not get involved in any activities. But if one aims to have a
rested life, serving God is one of the keys.

One of my greatest joys growing up in church was
serving God. I remember when I was as young as 8 or 9, I
would often look forward to go to church and serve. While
other kids were too busy with their TV's or whatever activities
kids were involved in during the 70s, I found it very refreshing
and joyous to serve in the house of the Lord. By the time
Monday arrived, I would be all ready to go (although not
necessarily excited about school itself, but I was very alert and
energized by Monday).

As an adult, before I became a full-time minister, I was
quite active in church as well. In my twenties, I went to church
every Friday evening to lead worship (I loved doing that) in
prayer meetings. And prayer meetings in those days went on
forever. After the prayer meetings were done, nobody wanted
to leave. I mean, we all just had a full day of work. You would

---

10 Matthew 20:28

think that we would all want to rush home and relax. Instead, people lingered on for another couple of hours. Why? You see, by the time we finished worship and prayer, we felt energized.

It would be close to midnight when I got back home from prayer meetings. As if that wasn't enough, I would often go back to church again the next morning to serve in various outreach ministries. It was not uncommon for me to stay at church until 9:00P.M. and then I'd back on Sunday for another day of worship and serving; yet, being there so much didn't feel like a drag. It was exciting and I loved every minute of it. By the time Monday would come around, I would be thinking about the next weekend with great anticipation.

By contrast, every Monday when I went back to work, I would see my colleagues looking exhausted. When I asked them what they were doing during the weekend that made them so tired, many would tell me that they had just spent the whole weekend doing nothing but enjoying some downtime. It would seem to me that relaxation and downtime didn't do anything to give them rest. Friends, when you truly serve the Lord from the revelation of how much God loves you, nothing is too hard, too tiring, or even too costly. When you find this true treasure of rest and fulfillment, you would even sell all that you have to get that rest.[11] When you come and serve the Lord, not out of bondage or guilt, but out of love for Jesus, God will give you rest in your spirit.

In Hebrews 4:2, we are told that the Israelites who left Egypt never really experienced the benefit (rest) that was intended for them because they never understood how to serve God. An examination of the book of Exodus reveals they tried all kinds of things except listening to what the Lord instructed them to do. They were called out of Egypt into the wilderness for the purpose of serving God. Instead they served something else.

A lot of people have been given the same freedom of rest. Yet instead of using that freedom to serve others, they would say to themselves, "Well I'm free now, so I don't have to do anything." And so, what do they do? They take the extra time to do something else, so when Monday comes, they are like everyone else. They feel very tired and exhausted, not only physically, but worse yet, they feel tired mentally and spiritually.

---

[11] Matthew 13:44-46

Friends, do you realize that the worldly system (like the Egyptian system of old) has figured out how to suck every ounce of energy from us? By Friday evening, people are usually exhausted. We work hard because we have bills to pay. By the weekend, it is rather natural that we want to stay home and relax. The devil tells us, "Don't go to church man, stay home like everyone else and just enjoy yourself." And so, we believe the lie. Yet, instead of resting, we find ourselves doing lots of other things that aren't all that relaxing after all. When we go to work on Monday morning, we feel as exhausted, unmotivated, burdened, and depressed as everyone else. I once heard somebody say, "We Christians should be quite different from people of the world." And I agree. I propose that one of the biggest differences should be seen in how Monday morning is handled. When everybody else is having a big cup of coffee to give them a boost (nothing is wrong with coffee, I love coffee too), we ought to be the ones with inner strength on display, with immense joy and hope. We ought to be so rested in our spirit that we are ready to take on the world.

Rest Through Sacrifice

The third thing God instructed Moses to tell Pharaoh was that He wanted His people to get out of Egypt so that they could make sacrifice unto the Lord. That speaks of our worship unto the Lord, especially when our worship is done sacrificially. What is worship? Worship is not just going to church once a while or once a week. Worship is not just singing or playing musical instruments. Worship is also giving sacrificially to the Lord on a consistent basis. In fact, the worship activities that are recorded in the Old Testament are mostly people of God bringing sacrifices/offerings (from the fruits of their labor) unto the Lord at the appointed time and places, consistently and faithfully.

Do you know that every sacrifice you make unto the Lord is an exercise to rest? Let's take offering (the most prevalent form of worship in the Bible) as an example. Offerings should not be an obligation. When we tithe, we tithe out of faith. Because the Bible says if we do anything not out of faith, it's a sin.[12] So, if we can't give out of our faith, then we may as well not give. But if we give out of faith, that is, if we

---

[12] Romans 14:23

believe the Word of God and step out in faith, God is going to take care of our needs. He's going to cause us to rest. When we give sacrificially as worship unto the Lord, He will give us Sabbath in our finances. What that means is that we will not have to worry about provisions ever again. Let's just think about that.

In the eighties and nineties, there was a financial company in Canada that advertised the concept of being financially free by the age of 55. They called it "Freedom 55"[13]. Unfortunately, not too many people were able to achieve the kind of financial independence and freedom this company proposed, especially at the young age of 55.

If we live by God's divine financial principles, such as giving sacrificially, above and beyond our tithe, we will experience true Sabbath in our finances. Money will no longer be an issue about which we ever need to be concerned. We will have true rest in our finances. Am I promising us all a million bucks? I am not. It may include a million dollars, but do you know that many who have a million dollars, or even multi-million dollars still do not find rest in their finances? That's

[13] Freedom 55 is a trademark of Sun Life Financial

why most millionaires still work very hard, not only to keep what they have, but to gain more, just as a guarantee. Why? They still worry. They worry that they might lose what they have. Many millionaires are up all night worrying about money!

What the Lord promises is this: if we bring Him the sacrifice of worship, He will give us rest. We will find rest in whatever we sacrifice to Him. We just spoke about money. How about our time? Are you feeling like you never have enough time? Friends, have you ever considered sacrificing your precious time to serve the Lord? I will guarantee you that you will find yourself having more time to rest! I can go on talking about many other areas of our lives in which we need rest, but I think you get the point.

His Presence Brings Rest

In Exodus 33:14, God told Moses, "My presence will go with you and I will give you rest." In other words, the presence of God brings rest. If you and I want to pursue true rest, we should make the pursuit of God's presence a priority. That is why Jesus is inviting His people, especially those who are heavy laden and burdened, into His presence. He says,

"Come unto Me, all you who are weary and carry heavy burden, and I will give you rest."[14]

Most of us lead a very hectic lifestyle. Not only do we have to work and toil at our job for at least 8 hours a day, many of us have to commute for a couple of hours a day as well. By the time we get home, we find ourselves absolutely exhausted; yet, we can't stop and rest because we have lots of chores at home to take care of. Some in my generation, which is also called a sandwich generation, not only do we have to take care of our children's well-being, but also that of our elderly parents. Consequently, we get very little or no rest, except for a few hours of sleep every night. To compound the restlessness even more, many of us also have sleep disorder (such as sleep apnea). With all this going on, it is not surprising when we break down either physically or mentally.

One of the best ways to rejuvenate ourselves constantly is to practice the presence of God by setting aside time to pray, even if it's only for a few moments. If we are able to practice His presence constantly throughout the day, we will find

---

[14] Matthew 11:28

ourselves feeling calmer and more rested even in the midst of great demands or trials.

One of the books that has helped me enter into God's rest all the time is called *Practicing His Presence*. This book is a compilation of various recorded conversations and letters of an 18th century monk by the name of Brother Solomon. (I am sure you are too busy to read that book; it's a miracle that you are reading this book, so I will try to summarize the content in a couple of sentences.) In this book, Brother Solomon shared about how he had cultivated the practice of God's presence so well that he could sense God's sweet presence every waking moment of his life. The sensation of God's presence was as pronounced as when he was working on jobs that he hated as when he was in his closet praying alone. Needless to say, this man was able to live a long life because he was able to be in that constant state of rest all his life.

Called to Gather Before Him

Practicing God's presence daily brings rest, but gathering with God's people in an assembly also brings a supernatural charge to our spirit, mind, and soul, especially when the Holy Spirit and His anointing are flowing freely in the assembly. I do realize that there are some church gatherings that are just going through religious exercises to appease the God who never asked them to do the things they are doing. Services in those churches are not only boring, but they are tiring and (in my humble opinion) just a complete waste of time.

There are a couple of reasons why so many continue to tolerate such dry church services. First, they think their religious exercise is the price to pay to please God, so that God would bless them. Religious institutions and leaders perpetuate the concept of boring, no-spiritual-power services to control people and keep them in fear. But nothing can be further from the truth of how things should be. Our services should be alive and anointed by the Holy Spirit because we are celebrating God's love, realizing His love for you and me does not increase or decrease based on what we do or don't do. Our excitement shows because He loves us and He sent His only Son to die for us because we are created in His own image,[15] and our lives are literally the breath of God![16] Even when we were yet sinners,

---

[15] Genesis 1:27
[16] Genesis 2:7

yes, even as His enemies, He died for us.[17] How much more for those who had chosen to accept Him as Savior and are now called sons and daughters of God!

The second reason many people continue to tolerate lifeless worship gatherings is because they believe it is a necessary evil to enjoy the fellowship/friendship of the community of believers after the service. In other words, the church is really a place that meets their social needs so people attend from week-to-week just to see each other, not to experience more-and-more of God.

Unfortunately, many dear saints do not realize that they are not being refreshed or re-energized by the presence of God. All they are doing in church is temporarily assuaging their guilt, or having their social needs met by their fellow believers. While it is not wrong to want to be in relationship, God has something else much more powerful in mind when He encouraged believers to gather.[18] What He intends for us is to have a true and powerful encounter with God. That's why He said, when we gather in His name (even in two's and three's),

---

[17] Romans 5:8
[18] Hebrews 10:25

He will be in our midst.[19] Why? Because His presence can bring so much more to our reality. His presence brings miracles, healings, signs, wonders, comfort, and assurance. Most of all, His presence brings rest to us all!

I remember, during the height of the revival at the Airport Church in Toronto (they have since changed their name to Catch the Fire Church), many people were attending the services every single night. Surprisingly, people did not feel exhausted or tired. A local newspaper interviewed a fellow who was there every day with the exception of Saturday, which was when he took a break. This fellow worked at six in the morning, and after work he rushed straight to that church. In those days you'd have to be there at least two hours before the service started, so that you could get in the front of the line to get the good seats. So, this man would rush to church and start lining up two hours before the service, at five o'clock. The services would go on and on until 11:00PM or even 12 midnights (depending on how long one stayed for prayer), and the man would then go home to get 3-4 hours of sleep before heading off to work again. When the reporter asked him,

---

[19] Matthew 18:20

"Aren't you tired? How long can you keep up with this kind of schedule?" The man told the reporter that he could keep going forever because he felt super-charged after each service. He said that he felt more hopeful, and he felt he had more strength and wisdom to do his work. He even said most people at his workplace did not know he was only sleeping for 3-4 hours, because he was more energized and happier! What happened? Well, the presence of God rejuvenated Him and gave Him supernatural rest.

Friends, when we spend time in the presence of God, we experience strength, joy, and hope. It's the kind of rest that will never come from just sleeping. In fact, many of us know that sleeping itself doesn't necessarily bring rest to the mind. It may give rest to the body, but the mind can still be racing on at 200 miles an hour. If we are depressed or discouraged, we may wake up still feeling this way after a night of sleep. However, when we spend time in the presence of God, He gives us His rest, His true and total Sabbath! This is not only a physical rest, but rest for our mind, soul, and spirit! You end up feeling recharged, and find your mind to be more alert, your soul more hopeful, and your inner man strengthened with more courage and joy! None of this can be found by just lying down horizontally. When we come to the presence of God and worship and bid His call as He asked the people of Israel, we will be renewed, refreshed, and totally rejuvenated!

When I first taught about rest in my congregation, some people thought that I was encouraging them to be lazy. Some even stopped coming to church, stopped serving God, and stopped serving others. They wrongly thought it was the will of God for them not to do anything, because God had called them to rest. If that were true, the people of Israel might still be in Egypt today! God's plan for His people to obtain true rest was calling them out from and separating them from the oppressive system of the world, and bringing them to His presence for five reasons: to feast before Him, serve Him, give sacrifices to Him, worship Him, and gather before His presence. As His people obeyed Him, not only did God refresh them, but He also brought supernatural rest in all the situations in which they were contending.

Chapter 5

Opposition to Your Rest

Now, the enemy of our soul, Satan, who is also known as the god of this world,[20] will use everything at his disposal to distract us from our rest or prevent us outright to reach that rest. If we have made the decision to live in the life of true rest, we can be assured that there will be fierce opposition to that decision. All kinds of distractions, like media, news, or different surprises will be thrown at us. As we will discuss later, the devil will keep hammering

---

[20] 2 Corinthians 4:4

at us until we are convinced (as an entire generation of Israel were) that rest is not worth the many troubles that come with it. But we must resist our enemy. Resist his distractions. Resist the troubles he is throwing your way. Resist the bad news. Resist the negative narratives. And as we do, we will find that one by one, all his oppositions will vanish (flee from you)[21].

Contending for Rest and Faith

While Hebrews 4:11 teaches us about rest, the entire book of Hebrews is actually a book about faith. In other words, in order for you and I to get into that place of rest, we need to have faith. Faith, and therefore rest, is what we must contend for and is what we must fight for.

Faith is what the people of Israel needed when they heard the call to come out of the yoke of Egypt and enter into God's rest. You see, when they first heard the good

---

[21] James 4:7

news, they believed and were glad. They thought rest would be handed to them on a silver platter and they had to do nothing for it. However, it turns out that they had to fight their way from the start in Egypt, all the way to the final destination of rest in the Promised Land. Let's look at the Bible's account of this time in the life of God's people:

"Then Moses and Aaron went and gathered together all the elders of the people of Israel. Aaron spoke all the words that the Lord had spoken to Moses and did the signs in the sight of the people. And the people believed; and when they heard that the Lord had visited the people of Israel. And that He had seen their affliction, they bowed their heads and worshipped".

Exodus 4:29-31 (NLV)

"Afterwards Moses and Aaron went and said to Pharaoh, "thus says the Lord, the God of Israel, 'Let my people go that they may hold a feast to me in the wilderness. But the King of Egypt said to them, "Moses and Aaron, why do you take the people away from their work? Get back to your

burdens." And Pharaoh said, "Behold, the people of the land are now many, and you make them rest from their burdens!" The same day Pharaoh commanded the task-masters of the people and their foremen, "You shall no longer give the people straw to make bricks, as in the past; let them go and gather straw for themselves. But the number of bricks that they made in the past, you shall impose on them, you shall by no means reduce it. For they are idle. Therefore: they cry, 'Let us go and offer sacrifice to our God.' Let heavier work be laid on the men that labour at it and pay no regard to lying words..... The foremen of the people of Israel saw that they were in trouble when they said, "You shall be no means reduce your number of bricks, your daily task each day. They met Moses and Aaron, who were waiting for them, as they came out from Pharaoh; and they said to them, "The Lord look on you and judge, because you have made us stink in the sight of Pharaoh and his servants, and have put a sword in their hand to kill us Because we've believed you. We believed what you had said. And now look at us"

Exodus 5:1,4-9, 19-21 (NRSV).

Moses told this to the Israelites; but they would not listen to

Moses, because of their broken spirit and their cruel slavery.

Exodus 6:9 (NRSV)

Here, we see that when the Israelites decided to accept God's invitation to leave Egypt and go to the place of rest, the devil did not sit back. Indeed, Pharaoh (no doubt moved by Satan) started to create opposition and increase his harshness on the Jews. So much so that those Jews were thinking of abandoning all hope of being free to serve God. It was becoming too hard to hope and believe in God's promises.

In the same way, friends, every promise of God to us will always be resisted by the enemy of our souls. Anything and everything that God would grant us will be met with great resistance from hell. In fact, as soon as we start to have hope in the promise of God, or start to believe in His Word, the devil himself will rev up the heat to intimidate us so that he can break our hope, break our spirit, and make us turn around and go back to unbelief and cynicism. That's what happened to the people of

45

Israel. They were so broken by their Egyptian masters that they decided not to listen to Moses anymore. They decided not to believe anymore. They were so intimidated that they no longer believed what Moses and Aaron told them about God giving them rest, or about how God is setting them free from the harsh yoke of slavery.

If we are going to make the decision to rest, to pursue that supernatural rest that He has promised us, there is a good chance that we will see a quick reaction from hell. Instead of getting rested, things may get harder and make us more restless. If we were in pain because of our sickness, the pain may become more pronounced. Instead of seeing improvement, we may feel like it's getting worse. Or, if we are starting to believe for rest in our finances by tithing and giving sacrificially, there may be some unexpected or surprise expenditures coming our way. This is how the devil intimidates and discourages those who start believing in God for things in their lives.

When we decide to challenge and resist failures, sickness, hardship, and everything else that steals our rest, we can expect a blow back from the devil. Some may say, "Oh no, I don't want a blow back, I'm afraid." But may I encourage you not to be afraid. Fear is from the devil! I am teaching you this so that we can all get prepared. There may come a time when the devil is going to put up a huge resistance towards your rest. But you need to know that God is always faithful. If you surrender to God and trust Him, He will always come through. If God can rescue His servants Shadrach, Meshach and Abednego from the great furnace fire,[22] He can and will also rescue you from your fire. If God saved Daniel from being devoured by the lions,[23] He can surely rescue you from whatever the devil will send your way.

The Word of God also says that even when Jesus found Himself in the darkest moments of His life, the Father sent angels to minister to Him, to give Him strength.[24] So, when you feel like you can't do it anymore, I guarantee you, God in His grace will send help to sustain

---

[22] Daniel 3
[23] Daniel 6
[24] Matthew 4:11, Luke 23:43

and uphold you!

Joy Gave Jesus Strength to Resist

Jesus indeed faced the most incredible resistance when He was trying to save the world. He was whipped. He was tortured. He was put on the cross and the Father turned His face away from Him.[25] How did He overcome such resistance? Hebrews 12:2 tells us that it was the joy that was set before Him that helped Him to endure the pain.

What does "the joy that was set before Him" mean? It means is that Jesus was able to see how His sacrifice would reconcile millions to the Father, would heal millions, and bring eternal life to millions. He imagined the joy that He would experience when He reaped the fruits of His sacrifice. That is what gave Him the strength to overcome hardship and whatever the devil threw at Him.

When the devil throws up resistance against us, we

---

[25] Matthew 27:45-46

must do the same thing. Imagine how our prayers would be answered and the joy we'd experience when those prayers were answered. So, if we decide to be at church every Sunday to worship God, the devil may use our boss to give us a hard time. We cannot get discouraged. Instead, we must keep pressing in for that rest, and imagine how we will be able to finally come to church and rest every Sunday without being asked to work. If the pain from our sickness gets worse after we start believing for healing, just imagine the joy that we will have when we are completely healed with no pain in our body. If we've started to tithe and give sacrificially, and the devil sends all kinds of unexpected expenditures, we cannot allow ourselves to be discouraged or complain. Instead, imagine the joy we will have when we are living in great abundance without fear of lack. What I am saying is this, when the enemy puts up resistance against our faith for rest, we mustn't give up. We must keep believing in the promises of God. Visualize the joy we will have when we experience those promises fulfilled.

The Battle to Rest

As believers, we are not called to strive in anything but for the goal of entering into His rest.[26] Even the several places where the Word of God tells us to contend or fight, they are not instructions for us to strive with stress until exhaustion. In fact, the few calls to battle are actually calls to enter into His rest. Take 2 Corinthians 10:4 for example. Here, Paul is calling the church to battle, not as the world would, using physical weapons fighting physical things or people. Indeed, the weapon of our battle is actually spiritual, and the target is removing bad ideas and changing mindset. What mindset? The mindset of the world, the mindset of slaves, the mindset of restlessness, the mindset of worldly pursuits, and all the other mindsets and ideas that would distract us from our rest in Christ.

---

[26] Hebrews 4:11

Chapter 6

Miracles on Your Way to Rest

¹⁰ So the LORD said to Moses, ¹¹ "Go in, tell Pharaoh king of Egypt to let the people of Israel go out of his land."

Exodus 6:10-11 (ESV).

⁸ Then the LORD said to Moses and Aaron, ⁹ "When Pharaoh says to you, 'Prove yourselves by working a miracle,' then you shall say to Aaron, 'Take your staff and cast it down before Pharaoh, that it may become a serpent.'" ¹⁰ So Moses and Aaron went to Pharaoh and did just as the LORD *commanded. Aaron cast down his staff before Pharaoh and his servants, and it became a serpent.* ¹¹ *Then Pharaoh summoned the wise men and the sorcerers, and they, the magicians of Egypt, also did the same by their secret arts.* ¹² *For each man cast down his staff, and they became serpents. But Aaron's staff swallowed up their staffs.*

Exodus 7:8-12 (ESV)

From the time Moses and Aaron stepped into the promise of God by faith, to the time the people of Israel entered the Promised Land, many, many miracles happened along the way. The scriptures we just read was the first of many miracles throughout their pursuit of rest. There were miracles to overcome resistance (put up by Pharaoh, the nations along the way to Canaan, and the people of Canaan), miracles of opening waters (the Red Sea and the Jordan), miracles of provision and health, miracles of the pillar of fire and cloud, and miracles of God's manifested glory (the dark cloud and great thundering and lightning.)

If we are contending for that promised rest, that supernatural rest, we will also experience miracles along the way to our goal. God is going to give us a few surprises on our journey to our rest. Why? So that He can prove to us that what He promised is true. So that He can affirm His Word to us. You see, generally speaking, miracles are very important for our faith. In fact, I would go as far as saying that miracles are essential for our faith walk.

In writing to the believers in Corinth, Paul the apostle reminded the believers that our faith cannot rest on words alone.[27] Those words need to be backed up by signs and wonders. Your faith and my faith cannot rest solely on what has been said or what has been written. Miracles confirm that God's words are truly being preached. We believe in miracles in my church not so that we can put on a show. We believe in miracles, we pray for miracles, and we celebrate miracles, because miracles

---

[27] 1 Corinthians 2:4-5

affirm to us that God is in our midst and what we preach is true. For Moses and Aaron, miracles were absolutely essential for them to accomplish what they were called to do: bring the people of Israel to the place of rest.

In Mark 16:20, after the disciples had received the Commission from Jesus to preach the gospel to all nations, the Bible tells us that "they went out and preached everywhere while the Lord worked with them and confirmed the message by accompanying signs" (NASB). In Hebrews 2:3-4, the author told us that salvation was first announced by Jesus our Lord, confirmed to us who heard Him and was affirmed by signs and wonders, and various miracles and by the gifts of the Holy Spirit, distributed to us by His will. So, you see, if the early church needed miracles, signs, and wonders to affirm what was being preached, we certainly need it more in our cynical culture. Be encouraged not to shy away from the experience of miracles, signs, and wonders; in fact, contend for it! Expect it! If you are attending a church where there are no miracles, you do have reason to question if what is being preached is truly from God.

I know that there are many preachers and churches who are known as Cessationists, who would have us believe that "completion" has come when the Bible was put together. They point to 1 Corinthians 13:8-10, which says that prophecies will fail and tongues will cease; therefore, they decided that miracles have also ceased. However, in that same passage, Paul also says that when completion truly comes, knowledge will cease. In other words, if what they say about gifts and miracles were true, then knowledge must also cease. Yet, these same Cessationists ignore that piece of logic, and continue to pursue knowledge by writing books, building Bible colleges, etc. But we know that completion has not yet come, because Jesus has yet to return. A new heaven and a new earth are yet to be; therefore, miracles, signs, and wonders continue to be available for those who believe. Don't be deceived by Cessationists, who are incredibly persuasive and are great communicators. They are good at manipulating and deceiving the masses about this truth.

Don't let them talk you out of miracles, signs, and wonders. Miracles, signs, and wonders are part of our inheritance!

If you are believing in God for certain promises, especially if you are believing God for rest, not only will God fulfill those promises, but in the process you will see confirmations of those promises through miracles, signs, and wonders as well.

Chapter 7

Strife Free Success

Do you realize that you and I were never wired to live the way we live in the modern economy? You and I were never created to live in a high pressure, fast paced, and exhausting lifestyle. In the old days when there was no electricity, people slept long hours because everything shut down after sundown. There was nothing to do except to rest. Historians say that as recently as the 1800s, sleeping time usually lasted for 12 hours, and there would be two sessions of sleep within a 12-hour time period.[28] That kind of sleeping habit was commonly known as the two-piece sleep. People would start with a 4-hour sleep, then wake up to read, drink some tea, or be involved in some other very leisure activities before going back to sleep again until the morning. People would only be active when there was daylight or sunlight. Not to mention the one day of total rest for God's people. Folks didn't have to work long hours and commute long hours like many working in big cities do these days.

Nowadays, we're living at a hectic pace! These days, we don't even get to rest after we've gone home from work. After working long hours, we still have things to do at night. In our modern society, we're considered "lucky" if we can put in six hours of sleep at night. Our lives, unfortunately, are full of strife. Many are sleep deprived from Monday to Sunday!

---

[28] At Day's Close: Night In Times Past by Roger Ekirch

Jacob, Isaac, and Abraham

Among Abraham, Isaac, and Jacob, I consider Isaac to be the most blessed. While Abraham and Jacob were very blessed, they both had to contend and strive for many things throughout their lives. Isaac, on the other hand, hardly did anything special. The only thing that was notable about Isaac is that he was put on the altar to be sacrificed and that wasn't even his decision. Yet he inherited all the wealth that Abraham had and got an incredibly beautiful wife with no effort of his own.

On the other hand, Jacob's life was especially tragic because he had to contend for a lot, more so than even Abraham his grandfather. I truly believe that Jacob could have been as blessed as his father and his grandfather without much strife because God had promised Abraham so much[29], yet he chose to strive. In his old age, after years of strife and heartache, he admitted that much. Recalling when he came to Pharaoh after discovering his son was

---

[29] Genesis 12:1, Hebrews 11:9

alive and now the Prime Minister of Egypt, Pharaoh asked him about his age. In response, Genesis 47:9 recorded what Jacob said, *"The years of my pilgrimage are a hundred and thirty. My years have been few and **difficult**, and they do not equal the years of the pilgrimage of my fathers."* (NIV).

Jacob felt like he was about to die. He was weak. Why? Because he had spent all his days striving. Friends, it is never the intention of God that we strive. It is His intention to bless us and He desires that we walk into the blessings. Jacob lived a shorter life than those who were ahead of him because his life was full of struggle. Why was he full of struggle? As I said, the blessing would have come to him as it had come to Abraham and Isaac without much strife. The answer is that he struggled because he was very ambitious.

My fellow believers, don't let your ambition drive you to the point of no rest, or to the point that may shorten your life. Scientists have confirmed that if we lose sleep, we will never be able to make up for it. We can't say, "I'm going to catch up on my sleep." It doesn't work that way. If we lose sleep, we lose it forever. All the sleep we lose could be contributing to the shortening of our lifespan.[30] Friends, you and I can certainly have great success by restlessly striving for it, but in doing so, we may not be able to enjoy our success for long.

Success Without Strife & Labour

Galatians 3:13 tells us that we have been "redeemed... from the curse of the law" (NIV). One of the great consequences of that redemption is that the the blessing promised to Abraham may come to us (Galatians 3:14). In other words, because we have no more curse to contend with, the blessing will flow into our lives without our having to work for it.

In John 4:35-38, Jesus was teaching about the

---

[30] "Diurnal Rhythms in Blood Cell Populations and the Effect of Acute Sleep Deprivation in Healthy Young Men," was a collaborative effort between the Department of Forensic Molecular Biology at Erasmus MC University Medical Center Rotterdam and Chronobiology, Faculty of Health and Medical Sciences at the University of Surrey, United Kingdom. The laboratory study was conducted at the University of Surrey Clinical Research Centre.

principles of harvest in the Kingdom of God. In that passage He spoke about the opportunity for great harvest being now, not four months from now or sometime later. Unfortunately, many church leaders have used this scripture to pressure believers to work and strive harder "for the Kingdom." Yet, the whole point of this teaching was not to strive harder, but to simply enter into the harvest (the blessings) without much labor. Listen closely to what Jesus says in verse 38, "I sent you to reap that for which you did not labor. Others have labored, and you have entered into their labor" (NKJ). In other words, Jesus is telling us that the opportunity for great blessings, great results, and in the context of His teaching, a great harvest of souls is now. Don't think that you need to wait any longer, or need to strive and labor more. Go and receive your harvest, receive your blessings, and bring the lost souls into the Kingdom. You are meant to reap someone else's hard work.

Whatever you are believing in God for, it's not the work that will bring great results and answered prayer.

Your "yieldedness", your obedience, and the rest you have in God's faithfulness will bring great results. Let God fulfill the dream He has given you.

Open Doors

Many of you have heard of the term "open door." It is a term that refers to how new opportunities become available without any hindrance. An open door could lead to a new opportunity to step into a greater season or a greater success and victory. An open door would bring you to a place where you were not able to go before. For example, receiving a new job opportunity is an open door. Getting a promotion is an open door. A business opportunity is also an open door. But did you know there are two types of open doors? One is the door that you pry open with your own strength, resources, blood, sweat, and tears. The other is the open door that you do nothing to open; you just walk through it. The latter is a much sweeter and more exhilarating experience. It is, in fact, the type of door that God wants us to walk through. God provides open doors that require no effort and strife of our own. He miraculously opens up doors for you. You may not even have expected them, but there they are, wide open doors for you to just walk right through!

Friends, many who had to pry their way through a closed door would attest that, even if they had made it through to the other side, the reality on the other side often falls far short of what they expected and hoped for. The grass was definitely not greener on the other side of a closed door.

Whether it's in relationships, your career, your ministry, your business or it's in your finances, I want to encourage you to rest in the promises of God and wait for your open door. Yes, do what you must to get yourself ready for this new season that is coming. Get your finances in order, get the right education, get yourself fit, etc. But do not try to force open any door yourself. Let God show you the way and lead you to the right open doors!

I know some of you may have been waiting for your open door for a long, long time. And you are getting impatient, so you are trying to make things happen. You keep banging on places where there is no open door. You may be wasting your time and energy trying to pry open or bang on doors that were never meant for you.

Recently, I was listening to a pastor bemoaning how his church couldn't grow. Although he had been at it for many, many years, he only saw a few people attending his church. I asked him, "Have you ever considered that pastoring that church may not be your calling?" I must admit, that was pretty bold of me to ask a question like that, especially when I know he is full of anointing in preaching and praying for the sick to get healed. He's also full of passion and power. Still I continued, "If you've been banging on this door for the past fifteen years and it hasn't opened, it's probably never going to open. Try another door. Who knows? It may be wide open and you may just walk through it."

Friends, do you realize that God has many open

doors that you and I never dreamed of or imagined. Sometimes we are so focused on the closed door that we miss the open door that was meant for us. I can tell you of many, many open doors I have experienced, those that I did nothing to open myself. The blessings on the other side are all so sweet. Why? Because I didn't labor for them!

Chapter 8

Chaos and Confusions

Read Exodus chapter 8 - chapter 11.

Whenever we as Christ-followers decide to do something good for ourselves—to exercise more, to eat better, to become better, to pursue God more, to believe for more, or to choose the lifestyle of rest—we will inevitably see chaos and disruptions.

When the people of Israel decided to follow God's path of freedom and rest, when they decided they would no longer tolerate the yoke of slavery, stress, and oppression from Pharaoh, chaos started to ensue. All of a sudden, the 10 plagues came. First, all the water in the country was turned into blood. Just imagine the inconvenience alone that surrounded this first plague. Even the most basic routines were now being severely interrupted: they could no longer wash themselves, do laundry, cook, etc. As if that was not tough enough, the-water-turned-into-blood disaster was immediately followed by a large invasion of frogs. Then there were gnats, followed by swarms of flies. From there, boils, hail, locusts, and darkness. Finally came the worst plague of all, the death of the first born of animals and men. These were horrifying disasters.

The point is, every time the Lord starts to do something in our lives, or every time there is a change or shift that God brings, we will see chaos. In fact, I would submit that during every physical or spiritual shift, there will be chaos. For the superstitious and fearful, chaos is judged as a sign that one is heading toward the wrong direction. But if we observe all the major shifts God brought about in the Bible, we discover they are accompanied by chaos in the beginning. Take the dispensation of Grace as an example. When God started to bring grace to humanity through Jesus' birth 2000 years ago, there was great chaos in the city where Jesus was born. Thousands of babies were slaughtered. Families were ruined. Great sorrow came.

It's like an earthquake. The reason the earth is shaking is because tectonic plates deep in the earth are shifting. The earthquake or the Tsunami that it brings (if the quake occurs in the ocean), is just the manifestation of what is being shifted or what has already been shifted; therefore, we should not be afraid or alarmed. We must not be like those who are superstitious and fearful. As men and women of faith, we need to understand that chaos is not necessarily a bad thing. In fact, it may very well be that God is bringing about the great shifts for which we have been longing and praying. Every seemingly major disaster, war, or seismic event is an indication of something that is shifting.

I say all of this to make this point: we may see chaos around us when we make the decision to pursue God's rest. When we decide to rest, we cannot be surprised if our tires get punctured, our heater stops working, or some other disruption gets us out of rest and back to strife and contention. When we are facing chaos in our lives, we must not give up on our decision to rest. We must take care of the things we need to take care of, but take care of them in rest. We cannot let our minds, our spirits, and our souls get out of rest.

Goshen Protection

In Exodus 8:22-23, we read, "But on that day I will set apart the land of Goshen, where my people dwell…" (RSV). In context, God was telling the people of Israel that even though they may see chaos and great disruption, they could trust that they will be protected. Notice, while the people of Israel were in Egypt, they did have to go through three of the plagues before they were spared.

What that tells me is that God will not always protect us from disruption and chaos that come about because of our decision to walk in His rest. Indeed, He will allow us to be tested through the trials, but only with what we can bear.[31] You may ask, why can't He protect us from all troubles, why does He allow any sorrow in our lives at all? Isn't He a good God? The answer can be found in James 1: 2-4 which says, "Count it all joy, my brothers, when you meet trials of various kinds, for you know that the testing of your faith produces steadfastness. And let steadfastness have its full effect, that you may be perfect and complete, lacking in nothing" (RSV).

According to the scripture we just read, testing and trials are meant to make us 1) Perfect, 2) Complete, and 3) Lacking in nothing. Without trials, believers become very dependent, cannot stand on their own, and are easily manipulated by circumstances. That is why James the Apostle encouraged his readers not to focus on disruption,

---

[31] 1 Corinthians 10:13

trials, and inconvenience, but to see the trials and chaos as opportunities to grow stronger in our faith. Nevertheless, our God is incredibly loving, in that He will never allow us to go through more than He had wired us to handle.

One more thing about His protection in the midst of chaos is this: His protection is conditional. Let me explain. Notice in Exodus 8:22-23, God promised His people that He was going to protect them in Goshen. In other words, only in Goshen will they find protection. If anyone of them were to step outside of Goshen, they would not have received the same protection. Also, during the last plague - the death of all first born - the people of Israel were commanded to paint their doorposts and lintels with lamb's blood; otherwise, their first born would be killed. In both of these examples, we see very clearly that our protection is secured only if we are found to be where we are supposed to be. Our protection is provided as we abide in God's instructions.

You may say, isn't God's grace greater than all sins? Yes, the grace to forgive us is greater than our trespasses.

The grace to heal us is greater than whatever sins we've committed. The Bible, however, never said anything about the grace to receive His protection regardless of what you do, including walking outside His Word and His will.

Just imagine this: what if in the camp of Israel, one or two of the Israelites tried to test their luck and go outside Goshen to check out the plagues? Do you think they would have been protected? Or what if during the night when the firstborn of all Egypt were killed, one or two families in the camp of Israel decided that it was too much of a hassle to obey all that they were told to do? Would their first born have been spared?

Now I agree that most of the religious rigmaroles are meaningless because they are but mere traditions of man. And I think that most people who observe meaningless rituals do so out of fear, or they are trying to please God. But, there are principles and guidelines in the Word of God that are not religious rigmarole and meaningless rituals. God's principles and guidelines exist to help us and protect us. We violate them at our own

Contending for Rest

peril.

We must remember that while the grace of God is indeed rich, and it covers all our sins and mistakes, there are always natural consequences to our actions and decisions. I have often used the example of someone jumping off the CN Tower.[32] Although the grace of God is there, and God forgives all our sins and trespasses, that grace nevertheless will not prevent that jumper from the CN Tower from becoming sidewalk pizza!

So, whenever we decide to walk in our own ways, and give no regard to God's Word, we do so at our own peril. We will be on our own. We will get hurt. God is not punishing us. He's not inflicting pain on us. It's just that now we're outside of His protection, His principles, and His covering of grace.

Take the Prodigal Son story as another example (Luke 15:11-32). Did that young man's father make him

---

[32] One of the tallest structures in the world, located on Front Street, Toronto, ON.

poor? Did his father make him stay with the pigs? Did his father cheat him out of his money? No. In fact, his father loved him and let him make his own decisions. So why did the son suffer? Because he chose to walk away from his father's protection. He suffered because he wanted to try out the world and the enticing lustful pleasures of the world. Guess what happened? He got robbed by the world after which he was seeking. He literally ended up with the pigs. Was his father trying to punish him? Of course not. The consequences of his own actions and decisions caught up with him. Nevertheless, when the Prodigal Son decided to repent and return home, guess how his father reacted? His father forgave him and never mentioned a word about his bad decision. Instead, his father put a robe on his back, a ring on his finger, and recognized him as his son as much as ever before.

What a picture of how our Heavenly Father treats us. Whenever we decide to repent and return back to His embrace, He will forgive us just as quickly as the prodigal's father forgave his son. And God will remember our bad decisions and wrong doings no more.

But even with all of this forgiveness, acceptance, and forgetting of the past, we may still have to experience the consequences of our own doings. Notice also that the father in the story did not go and look for his son or rescue him from the pigs. Nor did the father encourage him to return home. The son had to make his own decision to repent and return home. Only then did he experience his father's embrace.

Chapter 9

Compromise

As I mentioned earlier, whenever we make a decision for the better, we will face resistance and chaos. That is because the enemy of our soul never wants anyone to succeed in pursuing better things, especially the spiritual blessings that God has promised us. We will have a fight on our hands when we put ourselves in the position to receive God's rest. Yet, if we persist, we will also see another tactic the devil typically uses to convince us to rescind our decision to follow God's Words. That tactic is negotiation to get us to compromise on our decision.

That's what happened to the people of Israel when they wanted to leave the place of bondage and go and serve the Lord and rest in the wilderness. In Exodus 8:25, when Pharaoh realized that he may not be able to keep the people of Israel from serving God, he started to negotiate with them. First, he suggested that they could actually serve God and find rest inside Egypt. This stall tactic happens for us when the devil suggests that we can actually rest while we continue to subject ourselves to the yoke of slavery of the worldly system. Second, when that failed, Pharaoh then suggested that they should not go too far from their place of slavery. I can almost hear the devil saying the same thing to some of you about rest. That is, "Why so drastic? You don't really need that much rest. You don't really need to go to church on Sunday. Just work a little less. You'll be okay."

In Exodus 10:10-11, Pharaoh subsequently suggested that only the men should go, but they ought to leave their family and livestock behind. When Moses refused, Pharaoh then suggested that they can take their families with them, but that they should leave their livestock behind. Thank God, Moses did not relent to any of these ploys. Instead, Moses stood firm on his ground until the people of Israel were able to come to a total rest with their whole family and all their livestock.

You see, when we decide to pursue rest, we can be assured that not only will there be opposition, but there will also be the temptation to compromise. If we want to truly rest, we cannot allow even a hint of the yoke of slavery to be on us. We must press in fully to that rest. We will probably hear some voices saying, "You shouldn't be so extreme," or "God will only help those who help themselves," or "There is no such thing as total rest," or, "You have to do something or pay something," etc. All of these voices are attempts to make us compromise, and we just cannot allow ourselves to be swayed by any of them.

Partial Victory

Just as we ought to resist compromise, we also

should never settle for partial victory. Whatever it is we are pursuing, (in this case, we are pursuing rest), we must not settle for anything less than total victory. The devil may tease us with small victories (e.g., few hours off, or a weekend here or there), be we cannot settle for those counterfeits.

I know some of us would think, "Oh, but we've come so far. I guess that's good enough." Listen, whatever God has put in our heart, whatever dream He purposed or calling He put in us, the devil's intention is, first, to resist us all the way. If he fails at that, he will do his best to convince us to go only halfway. Imagine how Moses could have been tempted to take the offers of compromise from Pharaoh.

Friends, don't settle for partial rest. Don't settle just to go halfway. Go all the way. The Bible says that God will satisfy you with long life[33]. But if you're shortening your own life yourself through a stressful lifestyle, there's

---

[33] Psalms 91:16

nothing He can do. If you want to receive that promise of long life yet you still want to continue in your stress, how can God fulfill that promise in your life? It's like people who want to be healthy, but they keep smoking like a chimney and eat all the fat and sweet the world has to offer.

The other day while at the gym where I work out, I noticed that a number of other gym members were smokers. They would smoke before entering the gym and then smoke again after their workout. I thought to myself, *What a waste of time.* The predicament faced by the smoking gym members is the same as the one faced by believers who desire health and long life, yet they disregard living a healthy lifestyle. Yes, God wants to heal us and give us long life, but if we are doing everything to the contrary, miracles or not, we won't have a long life. Miracles of God are not meant to enable us of our irresponsible behavior.

You cannot let the world tell you that it's okay to sleep for six hours a night and work for fourteen hours every day. Reject that in Jesus name. You may say, "My boss is like that." Well, start looking for a new job. Don't settle for being a slave. It's commendable to be diligent, hardworking, faithful, and not lazy. Remember you are not a slave! For it was for freedom Christ has come and set us free. God intended that you be free from all the yokes of slavery, from the world and from the devil himself! If you feel enslaved, get out! Slavery does not bring about rest.

A really good friend of mine actually works sixteen hours a day and he's boasting about it. He's not too much older than I am, but he looks like he could be my father. Did you know that Jesus also slept? Some say, "No, he prayed all night." Yes, there were times when He was called to pray all night, but that did not happen most of the nights of His earthly life. When He needed to sleep, He slept, even in the boat that was about to sink![34] That's a gift brothers and sisters. Rest is a gift. Don't let the devil steal that gift from you. Don't let your work steal that rest. Don't let electronics steal that rest. Don't let your worldly possessions steal your rest. And don't let pride and

---

[34] Mark 4:35-38

ambition steal your rest.

I believe the fight for rest is the fight of the century. This message of rest is so contrary to our culture. Our culture hates rest. What it promotes as rest is just a couple of weeks relaxing on a beach. That's not rest. That's a deception. Because by the time you get to the fifth day, you'll be thinking about work again and all the headaches that are going on in your workplace and life. Friends, God wants to give you rest that is permanent and constant. When you're fully at rest, you're free to serve, to love, to live, and to enjoy all the blessings of God. That's your portion. That's the promise of God.

Chapter 10

Sojourning

Read Exodus 14:1-29 and Numbers 13 & 14

When God led the Israelites out of Egypt, one of His main purposes was to call out His people to a place of *permanent* rest. God had never intended that they would sojourn forever in the wilderness. The wilderness experience, nevertheless, was absolutely essential. I recently heard a well-known preacher put it this way: "God never leads us to the wilderness if there is no *promised land* on the other side."[35]

Today the call to rest is still the same. God's call for us is not so that we can rest one day a week, or rest temporarily like a sojourner. What He is calling us to is a place of permanent rest. He is calling us to develop that mindset of rest and therefore a spiritual lifestyle of rest. We can enter that place of rest all the time. What that means is that there will be no stress in our thought life, no stress in our soul, and our spirit man is continually at peace. Regardless of what chaos, disaster, or unexpected turbulence the devil may throw at us, we are still able to be in rest. But, this call to a spiritual lifestyle of rest can't be achieved overnight.

The Longer Route (As Opposed to Shortcuts)

As in any good lifestyle (i.e. a healthy lifestyle) a spiritual lifestyle of rest must be cultivated and intentional.

---

[35] iBethel.tv Podcast. Speaker: Bill Johnson

This means we must be willing to go through the process of learning, resisting temptation, and growing.

Now, let's look back again at the journey of Israelites in chapter 14 of Exodus. If we look at the map of the Middle East, specifically at the span between Goshen of Egypt and Canaan, we will quickly realize that the distance between these two regions would not take 40 years to cross. In other words, if the people of Israel had traveled from Goshen, by the coastal seas of the Mediterranean Sea (also known as the "Way of the Philistines"), they would have reached the Canaan land in twelve and a half days. Putting it in our modern measurement, the distance between Egypt and Canaan by that route is about two-hundred miles, a mere three-hour drive on a regular North American highway!

Now humans on average walk 3.1 miles per hour. If you factor in all the livestock, the children, and so forth, they may have walked slower, perhaps 2 miles an hour. Based on that conservative assumption, it would therefore take them around one hundred hours or 12 ½ days to walk from Goshen to the Promised Land.

Instead, God told Moses to lead the Israelites through the longest route possible, which was going first to the southernmost part of the Sinai Peninsula, and then going all the way back up the same peninsula before entering Canaan land.

Interestingly, even if you travel the long way (two hundred miles), it still would have taken the people of Israel only less than 100 days to walk. How do I know that? Again, using the math from above, 200 miles/2 miles per day = 100 days. Using the scripture, we can also deduce the same result. As you know, the people of Israel received the 10 commandments of the Lord at Mount Sinai. And we know that the time they received the commandment of the Lord was fifty days from when they first left Goshen. How do I know it's fifty? Well, because the day they received the 10 Commandments of God is also known as the day of Pentecost. And we know that Pentecost (Penta, fifty) is literally 50 days after the Passover (the night before they left Egypt.)

Again, as we observe the map, we see that the distance from Mount Sinai to Canaan land is almost the same as the distance from Goshen to Mount Sinai. Therefore, if it took them 50 days to travel from Goshen to Mount Sinai, it should therefore, have taken them only another 50 days from Mount Sinai to the Promised Land, a grand total of 100 days. Yet instead of one hundred days, God led them around and around for forty years before they reached the Promised Land. A three-month journey took them forty years!

So why did God allow a 100-day journey to take 40 years? Why does God prescribe the longer way? The immediate reason was because of their unbelief and resistance against taking the land God said was theirs. They allow fear and their slave mindset to reject the Word and promise of God.

But friends, if God is leading us to travel the longer route, it must be for very good reasons. I contend that there are three additional reasons for their long trip mentioned in Exodus because God's foreknowledge saw their needs. God realized their trials could make them change their minds, their victories would be difficult to maintain without training, and their faith needed to be built.

Trials and Temptations

The first reason for the longer route is explained in Exodus 13:17:

> *"When Pharaoh let the people go, God did not lead them by the way of the land of the Philistines, although the way was near. For God said, "Lest the people change their minds..."* (RSV).

You see, God anticipated that the Israelites would be tested in their faith and therefore change their mind and decide to return back to their old ways of living in slavery. Sometimes we too may find ourselves being led through the longer route.

Do you know that God knows our weaknesses? He knows what we can handle and He knows what we can't handle. He's not a cruel God. He's not going to put us through situations where the devil would have an upper hand.

In 1 Corinthians 10:13 we read:

"No temptation has overtaken you that is not common to man. God is faithful and He will not let you be tempted beyond your ability, but with the temptation, He will provide a way of escape that you may be able to endure it" (RSV).

So every single time when there is a temptation, when there is a trial, when there are some challenges ahead of you, or when there is a circumstance that would challenge your faith, you can rest assured that if you can't handle it, God will provide a way for you to avoid it.

This is what He was doing here with the people of Israel. You see, God knew that the Israelites could be easily intimidated. The prospect of facing their enemies in warfare, even giants, was too overwhelming for the recently released slaves. So, instead of letting them confront the enemies early on, in His loving wisdom, God led them through another way until they were more ready to face the challenges.

In our lives, we often become impatient with God when in His eternal grace and mercy, He seems to be leading us through a longer way to our goal. You see, the key is to wait on the Lord and follow His leading. God's answer to our prayers may not be in the timing that we imagine because He sees the obstacles that lie ahead which may overwhelm us. Don't be in such a hurry. When we're in a hurry, we tend to run ahead of God and get ourselves into trouble.

Training to Ensure Victories

The second reason why God led the people of Israel via the longer route was to train them so that they could experience victories. Training takes time. If they had gone into the Promised Land right after they left slavery, they would have been slaughtered by the inhabitants of the land. While God often wants His people to sit back and watch how He would deliver them miraculously and give them victory entirely with His grace, there are also times that He wants His people to experience the joy of having faith and victory through partnering with Him. The journey of Israel to rest, I believe was the latter. That leads me to my third point.

Faith for Champions

Now, the third reason for God to lead the people of Israel via the longer route can be found Hebrews 4:2:

> *"For good news came to us just as to them (i.e. the people who were mentioned in Exodus), but the message they heard did not benefit them (that would be the message of rest), because they were not united by faith with those who listened"* (RSV).

In other words, they did not have faith. Another translation says that they did not mix what they heard with faith. The reason was very simple: they had no faith to begin with! As slaves, they did not know faith. All they knew was fear. Their Egyptian taskmasters used fear to govern them and drive them. So, God needed to train them in their faith. For them to succeed as conquering champions, they needed to learn how to live by faith and not fear. Unfortunately, many believers today are also living their Christian walk by fear. They make decisions in life out of fear. They even serve God out of fear. Fear, my dear friends, are how slaves have been conditioned to live. But you and I are children of the Most High. Fear is never from Him![36] If it is not from God, guest where fear comes from? The Devil, the enemy of your soul!

Training of Faith

One of the biggest confusions I had while reading Exodus 14 is how God intentionally hardened Pharaoh's heart. It sounds like God was trying to bait Pharaoh. It was as if God was saying to Himself, "Okay, if I do this,

---

[36] 2 Timothy 1:7

Pharaoh is going to go for the bait. So, I'm going to use the people of Israel as bait." It sounds like God was rather cynical and was trying to play games here! It sounds like God gave no value to the lives of the people of Israel, but just wanted to demonstrate His power!

Now if you remember the story, as a consequence of them following God to the wilderness, the Israelites found themselves trapped with no obvious way to escape.

> *"As Pharaoh approached, the Israelites looked up, and there were the Egyptians, marching after them. They were terrified and cried out to the Lord. They said to Moses, "Was it because there were no graves in Egypt that you brought us to the desert to die? What have you done to us by bringing us out of Egypt? Didn't we say to you in Egypt, 'Leave us alone; let us serve the Egyptians'? It would have been better for us to serve the Egyptians than to die in the desert"*

> Exodus 14:10-12 (NIV).

If I were in their shoes, I too would be scared and angry. I would probably be one of those who complained and murmured against Moses. It would be rather tough not to worry. But the truth is this: God was setting them up so that their faith could be trained.

As we continue in the story, we see that God delivered all of the Israelites without a single casualty. They witnessed the most amazing miracles before their eyes. God was gracious to them, even as they were complaining, because He understood them. You see, sometimes we are put in a situation where we do not understand the "why," so we complain. But because God understands us well, and knows that we need to be trained, He still graciously brings miracles to our lives to help us. I believe that the more miracles we experience, the more we learn how to trust Him.

To summarize, in order for us to increase our faith and trust in God, and therefore increase our rest, there have to be opportunities for our faith to be trained. The more training, the better. Our faith doesn't just grow by itself, or by our wishing and wanting it to grow. Our faith needs challenges and resistance not just once or twice, but throughout our life journey, so that our faith can grow. That's what the Apostle James said in James 1:2-4:

> *"My brethren, count it all joy when you fall into various trials, knowing that the testing of your faith produces patience. But let patience have its perfect work, that you may be perfect and complete, lacking nothing"* (NKJ).

That is why the people of Israel were led to face many challenges and oppositions. And each time God provided a miracle for those challenges. It was the insurmountable challenges coupled with those miracles, signs, and wonders that caused their faith to grow.

As an analogy, think of people who work out and do resistance training. Their muscles do not appear all by themselves. Unless those people train and work hard, they won't see any progress. If they go to the gym and don't exert any energy or put in an effort, they will never develop any muscles. In fact, the way to properly build muscles is to push or lift the weights until one can't push or lift anymore. Muscles will only develop at the point you give it your last bit of energy.

In our context, every time there is a resistance to your faith, it pushes your faith to grow. Your faith will increase ever more so when you experience miracles at the end, you will be ready for them. I tell you, I've gone through many trials saying, "God, where are you? You know, I thought I obeyed you. And yet, here we are. I want to quit. I don't want to do this anymore!" Then a miracle would come through, and I would have to say, "Oh sorry Lord, I spoke too soon." But you know what? Through the struggle and the wait, my faith grew and I learned to trust in God more. So, whenever you face resistance, instead of bemoaning to God about the challenges, do what James encourages us to do, count it all joy![37]

Importance of Faith

Why is faith so important? Friends, you cannot rest

---

[37] James 1:2-8

unless you can trust. You cannot trust unless you have faith. In order for you and I to enter into true rest, we need to trust God, even in the direst circumstances. That trust can only come when we have developed the kind of faith that believes that God is good all the time, and that He is faithful even when we don't see it right away.

A number of years ago, our church was experiencing some financial difficulties. It was not the first time, but this time seemed to be more pronounced. Now if you have been to our church, you would know that I never push for money. I will teach about giving and finances, but not with the intention of raising money. I will teach the principles of giving for the benefit of the listeners. I will teach about giving and offerings so that the people can experience the grace and miracles of God in their finances.

Well, here we were, and our church finances were running deficits by over ten thousand dollars a month. At that time, we only had less than 100 people in our congregation. While we had some funds in reserve, we were concerned about the possibility of needing to borrow money before too long. And if you are part of Willowdale, you know that I never want to be in debt. Since my personal conviction is to never be in debt (neither personally nor as a church), I had to inform the board about what was going on; however, I asked that they keep the information to themselves in prayer. So, we waited, prayed, and trusted God. We saw the bank balance kept going down drastically every month until it was almost empty! You can imagine how I felt. Then one Sunday, out of nowhere, a couple in our church who did not know about the financial situation gave the church $30,000.00. They didn't even attend regularly!

After that initial inflow, money continued coming in. Before we knew it, the church grew and so did our finances. Since then, we have experienced similar financial challenges, but through each time, our faith grew. Today we don't even worry about finances anymore. God continues to supply miraculously to our church. We have learned how to rest in God in our finances because we have learned how to trust in His provision.

For the many pastors out there, I would like to encourage you to test God in this area of finances. If you've been called to minister, learn to trust God as your provider. If you look to people to provide, you're going to have a short life because you are going to be under a lot of pressure. Inevitably, you're going to have to pressure people to give in your church. And if you do, don't be surprised that they leave your church. Friends, giving is always between believers and their God. As pastors, you have to learn how to trust in God's provision. I always challenge preachers not to preach faith so that they themselves don't have to live in faith. People in their congregations have no one to turn to for money, why then are you turning to them for money with guilt, pressure, and condemnation? Often, I hear ministers exhort people during offering time to "give in faith." That's a good exhortation; however, if the ministers' motivation is to collect more money so that they don't really need to trust God, then the exhortation sounds very hypocritical.

I know this is very difficult. I struggled with this for a number of years. I would complain to the Lord, "God, You're no provider. You're not good. We should just forget it." Sometimes, I had even become very skeptical. But after a few rounds, my faith grew stronger. Now, I don't even look at the money anymore.

But I digress.

Using this "Trust and Rest" principle, we can learn to grow in faith. Challenges in your life are opportunities for your faith to grow, whether those challenges are financial, relational, or in some other areas. You may even fail sometimes, but by facing the challenges, trusting God, and resting in His ability to provide, I guarantee that you will grow. When your faith becomes mature, you can truly rest in the Lord.

I remember when I was younger in ministry, the church I pastored had about thirty to forty people attending our Sunday services regularly. I used to worry about attendance every Sunday. I didn't only keep attendance every Sunday, but would use computer tools to chart graphs and do analysis. The more I look at those charts, the more discouraged I became. I tell you, tracking that attendance was more stressful than when I was a sales manager in the high-tech industry. When the Lord taught me to trust in Him, I stopped counting. People ask me why I stopped counting. My answer was very simple: I needed to trust God and listen for instructions from Him. And guess what? As soon as I stopped counting for attendance and checking data the church grew all by itself, just as His Word has said![38] Glory to God!

---

[38] Mark 4:27

Chapter 11

The Road Less Travelled

In Numbers chapters 13 and 14, we learned that the people of Israel had finally arrived at the edge of the Promised Land. Moses sent twelve spies into the land. Those twelve spies went in and looked at the land, and lo and behold, it was exactly what God had described it would be like.

I want to tell you this, whatever God has promised you, He will always confirm. You can send spies, or you can do whatever you want to do to make sure, but He will never fault you if you try to seek confirmation of His promise.

Anyway, the twelve spies sent out by Moses came back and basically said, "Yeah it's true. The land is fantastic," but ten of them also said, "but we can't conquer it." The other two said, "Sure, yes we can conquer the land because God says for us to do so. We're not taking it because of our ability, but because God says so. We can go." Then the naysaying ten said, "No, we can't take the land because we look like grasshoppers compared to those inhabitants of the land."

This is what the devil wants to do. He wants us to focus on us and our weaknesses. Instead, God wants us to focus on His promises. When we focus on ourselves, the task seems overwhelming and impossible. But each time when we focus on the promises of God, our faith gets stronger.

In the Biblical account we're now considering, we learn that Caleb and Joshua were the only two from their generation who got into the Promised Land. Why?

Because they were the two spies who focused on the promises of God. They acted in faith: Because God says so, we can do it! The rest of the ten spies reasoned, "No, we can't do it. We don't care what God says. Logically it doesn't make sense. We can't do it."

Unfortunately, the rest of the camp of the Israelites decided to side with the majority. You see, this majority rule thing doesn't work when it comes to a faith decision. Do you realize that at any given time in the history of humanity, only the minority sees the truth? Only the minority sees the revelation. Even Jesus warned us that there are two ways: one way leads to destruction; the other way leads to life everlasting. That way to life everlasting is far less traveled than the way to destruction.[39] Why? Because the way to everlasting life is narrow. Why is it? Because many people do not want to walk through the road that is difficult. Most want to walk through the wide road because it's easy, and most folks love what's easy.

---

[39] Matthew 7:13-14

The bad news is that when they walk through that easy road, they eventually find destruction. So, don't feel so bad in terms of your faith in Christ, in terms of your faith in God. Don't feel bad if you are the only one in your circle of influence that believes in entering God's total rest while you are still alive on Earth. Don't feel bad because you are in the minority. You are in the right club! The club of minority! God always manifests himself in the club of minority.

Well, the entire camp of Israel decided to believe in the majority of the spies. Instead of obeying the command of God and believing in His promise, they chose to disobey God and resist His promise. That resistance made God so mad that He promised that everyone 20 years old and older (except Caleb and Joshua) would never enter into the Promised Land. None of that generation except two would ever enter into that rest.

When the Israelites realized they had disobeyed God out of their fear and unbelief, and that God had rejected them, they changed their minds, but it was too late for them. Instead of obeying God and returning to their desert wanderings, they again disobeyed God and decided to try to possess the land on their own. Off they went. Guess what happened? Tons of them got slaughtered.

Now, this is another point I am trying to make. The first time when God sent the Israelites through another way, it was because God saw they were not ready. The second time, however, was not because they were not ready, it was because of their unbelief! They did not believe what God said about them: that they were ready.

God said they were victors. God said they were conquerors. God said they were victorious. God said they would be overcomers. God said that the promise was true and He had it ready for them. God said they could do it! Instead of believing God, rejoicing in Him, and obeying His Word, His promise, and His proclamation, the Israelites rejected God in unbelief. Consequently, they missed God, and were never able to enter into His Promise, His rest!

Today, many people have heard God's Word saying that He has forgiven them, they are the righteousness of God, they are victors, they overcomers, they are not full of defeats, and they are victorious to enter into His rest. Yet many are still convinced that they will never measure up, never be good enough, and never be accepted by God, so they keep striving and striving to be better, both in the world and even in church.

One of the reasons why many cannot accept this incredible invitation of God to accept His grace and goodness is the many years of false religious teachings that have convinced people that they are never good enough. False teachings have conditioned people to focus on the failures of men and their inability to meet the high standard of God. I want to remind you that you are not to look at yourself. You must look only to the promises of God in Christ and His atoning works. Look to the promise that says you are a victor because Christ is the Victor. Focus on the promise that says you are an overcomer because Christ has overcome. Remember the promise that you are the righteousness of God[40] because Christ has taken all your sins upon Himself. When you can believe all these truths, you can then rest. Otherwise you will be laboring not only in your job and personal life, but you will also be laboring to please God. The key is this: You have to focus on God and His promises, not on yourself!

I promise you, when you believe in the Word of God, you'll do things that are totally amazing. You will be surprised at what the Lord can do through you while you are at rest, and you will surprise a lot of the people around you.

New Generation, New Mindset

Now, because the people of Israel refused to listen to God's Word and therefore refused to believe what God said about them, they had to wait for forty years before they got another chance to get their land. In fact, none them made it except Caleb and Joshua. God had to wait

---

[40] 2 Corinthians 5:21

for an entire generation of "unbelievers" to pass away before He could bring that nation into their promise. He had to wait for a new generation who were not influenced by the unbelieving old generation so He could do His work.

This is not unique only to those unbelieving Israelites in the desert. Do you realize that Christians throughout the history of the Church had also behaved the same way? That's why the revival history of the Church is littered with similar examples of how God needed to wait until one generation passed before He moved onto the new generation? Why? Because more often than not, many of the older generations that had been conditioned by an old religious mindset had often rejected the new move of God with unbelief. The older generation would criticize and judge the new generation, and in fact, calling the moves of God that were unfamiliar to them heretical.

You know, we Christians often call ourselves conservatives. You know what that means? Narrow-mindedness! It's a good thing to be narrow-minded about the standard of God, about His Word, and about His truth. But we should never be narrow-minded about a new move of God, a new working of the Holy Spirit. Often, when God is doing something new that is foreign to us, we should not be so quick to reject it, shut it down, or persecute it. We should always be open-minded to new ideas.

When we're not open-minded, God cannot move. If we're so fixated on whatever theory we have about ourselves, about the move of God, and about the manifestation of God, God can't move. But when we are willing to come to that place where we are very open, we will see new and greater things happen.

See, the reason God often seems to be waiting for a new generation for His new move is because the new generation has no idea what their parents went through nor how they had been conditioned. For the people of Israel, the new generation did not know anything about slavery. They did not have the mentality of a slave. They were told that they were so special and the God of the Universe Himself would fight for them. So, they just have a different mindset. Their mindset is more open, so God can use them and can move through them and bring them to rest!

As for their parents, while they were delivered from slavery, the mindset of slavery never got removed out of them. They still thought like slaves and talked like slaves. They were still as insecure as slaves. That's why they could not believe they could overcome the inhabitants of the land. If they were to look to God, focus on His promise, and shake off the influences of where they came from or how they may have been viewed by their Egyptian master, they may have believed that they could be conquerors and overcomers. In spite of all the miracles God gave them, the slaves in their hearts never got set free.

You and I need to make the decision not to allow slavery to continue in our hearts. We got to pray that God would remove the idea of ourselves as slaves: slaves to our mortgages, slaves to our bills, slaves to our employers, slaves to the systems of this world, slaves to our past mistakes, or slaves to those of whom we are fearful.

Many of us have parents who are a part of the "baby boomer" generation. That generation had experienced tremendous lack and poverty; consequently, they worked really hard and encouraged their children to work hard, so that they would never see that kind of poverty and suffering again. For them, even Christians in that generation, the idea of rest is a fallacy. Not only must they slave away for a better life, but they also have the same mindset about their salvation and their place before God. I pray, however, that God will help us not to think like that generation, but receive His promise of rest and freedom as gifts. Believe that you don't need to be a slave most of your life. You are free: free to live, free to serve God, and free to be in rest.

In the city I live in, there are many immigrants who have come from all over the world (over 50% of the population here were not born in the city.) When they were in their native countries, many went to university and became successful in their chosen fields (i.e. doctor, accountant, lawyer, police officer, or even politicians.) But when they came to Canada, they were not able to quickly find opportunities in their chosen professions and ended up doing menial work for very little pay. Worse yet, many of their fellow countrymen discourage them and tell them that this is the reality of all immigrants. Many believed those lies and settled in meager jobs completely disillusioned about life in Canada.

In my church, there are many of these amazing immigrants from all over the world, and I have often encouraged them that God did not bring them here to fail, but He brought them here to succeed. He did not bring them here to be slaves, but He brought them here to manifest His goodness to all the world. Indeed, we have witnessed many immigrants in our church who are now succeeding incredibly well. The key was in their willingness to change their mindset from the mindset of a slave to a mindset of a son. They are sons of the Most High! We must believe that we are never called to be second class, living only to become someone else's footstool!

Unfortunately, for the people of Israel that had come out of Egypt, that mindset of slavery never left them despite all of the grace and goodness God had demonstrated to them. Many Israelites asked, in fact, begged to go back to Egypt and becoming slaves again. Some even asked to go back while standing at the precipice of realizing the promise of God which was permanent rest in abundance!

Chapter 12

Under the Light

"And they moved on from Succoth and encamped at Etham, on the edge of the wilderness. And they went before them by day in a pillar of cloud to lead them along the way and by night in a pillar of fire to give them light, that they may travel by day and by night. The pillar of cloud by day and the pillar of fire by night did not depart before the people" Exodus 13:20-22 (RSV).

In this passage, we see another example of the grace of God that leads people into true rest; He will always bring clarity in our journey. You see, when there is darkness, there is confusion. When there is confusion, strife and restlessness ensue. God will never lead us walking in the dark. Darkness is confusion. Unfortunately, many people in our society today are living in darkness.

There is a lot of confusion out there. They can't see any clarity in anything, let alone rest. Why? Because they are far from the light. Why? They've decided to walk away from the light. They allowed the many temptations, theories and arguments to lead them away from the Light. Allowing these things to happen would be like the people of Israel walking away from that pillar of fire. We're supposed to follow the light, not have the light follow us! It's illogical to walk away from the light in favor of walking in darkness and confusion.

If you find yourself restless and confused, there is a good chance that you have swerved away from the Light of God and walked in your own way. Just pause and look for that pillar of light. Look at that pillar of fire, and go to the place of the pillar of fire. Don't settle in darkness and continue to struggle and struggle and struggle. You're not meant to be in confusion. You're not meant to be struggling all the time. You're meant to walk in clarity. That's why God gave the Israelites that pillar of fire. And God has also given us a pillar of fire. Do you know where it is? It's where His people are congregating. The people of Israel always moved and congregated where the pillar of cloud and fire were, so the people of God today congregate around His presence. The good news is that God is not mad at us. He is waiting for us to return to His presence, to His Word, to His House, and to His leading. We can walk out our life journey in great clarity. When there is clarity, again, our soul will be at peace and in rest.

Protection and Comfort

Not only did God supply the pillar of fire by night, but He also provided a pillar of cloud by day. That pillar of cloud was meant to provide protection from the raging hot sun. Instead of travelling under the intense heat of the sun, God provided them that pillar of cloud for protection and comfort. It was like a super, giant-sized canopy over them, so that they could walk out their journey in comfort.

Do you realize that it is God's desire that we too walk out our life journey under His protection and in His comfort? So many people, even many sincere believers miss this. They think being spiritual is to be hard on oneself. They think the more we are in torment, the more God is impressed with us. That's a religious mindset. Not unlike all the other religions of the world insist that it's necessary to be in some kind of discomfort or even pain to please their gods. But that's not in the character of the God we serve. The God of the universe whom we serve loves us so much that He wants to make sure that not only are we protected, but we also are comforted. Are there seasons of training or even pain? Sure there are, but remember, while He allows the tragedies, misfortunes, and vicissitudes of life to train us, He is never the author of bad things. Why? Because He is a good God, and He can't do bad things.

If you find yourself in a place of great discomfort and pain, run back to His presence, run back to the

"Pillars of fire and Cloud". So that you can hearken unto the voice of your God. Come to Him and He will give you rest.[41]

On the other hand, don't run ahead of God either. Again, follow that pillar of fire or that pillar of cloud. Don't run ahead of those pillars.   Just because you cannot handle your work environment, doesn't mean that you need to rush out of that place. Don't go and quit your job and say God is telling you to rest before seeing God opening the door for you. It may not be the time yet. Perhaps you also need to get ready for that rest by saving enough money to support yourself before quitting; otherwise, you may find yourself running out of money, and not able to meet your obligations.

We need to wait on God. He will open the way. He will give you the right and perfect timing. He may have a job waiting for you. Now if God really spoke to you, then you need to obey His voice by faith. But if you're not too

---

[41] Matthew 11:28

sure, He is not going to send judgement to you just because you're not too sure. If you're not too sure of the decision, then don't make it. I've often said that, "unless you have confirmation after confirmation after confirmation after confirmation, don't make decisions you could soon regret." Our God is not a monster. He doesn't want you to second guess His command. He's not a God who would whisper in another room and expect you to hear His voice and obey 100%.

So, if you're not too sure of a particular decision, just wait and hold on. I want to encourage some of the young people to develop the discipline and the character to wait. This is the best discipline you can cultivate for your life because as you learn to wait upon the Lord, He will give you clear signals, open doors for you, and help you to avoid pitfalls and setbacks.

Chapter 13

Sight and Focus

Read Numbers 13 and 14.

In Numbers chapters 13-14, we read that the people of Israel had finally come to the place of promise, and they were about to take possession of what had been promised to them by God. However, due to what they saw was an impossible obstacle—the current inhabitants of the land were big and they felt like they were just like grasshoppers in their own eyes—they refused to follow through and get what God had for them.

If you are like most people in the world, you probably feel the same way regarding the promise of rest. You probably think it's impossible to live in the lifestyle of rest. There are too many bills to pay, children to look after, parents to care for, and all kinds of other obligations and expectations to handle. You probably think it won't be until you are fully old and retired before you get to that place of rest. The obstacles to living in the lifestyle of rest are too great. Friends, may I encourage you not to focus on the obstacles that prevent you from rest. Instead, focus on the promises of God that you can indeed be at rest.

You see, that's the trick of our enemy! He often prevents believers of God from obtaining their promises by making them focus on the obstacles, especially those right in front of them. However, whenever believers learn to focus on the promises of God and God Himself, they will see and experience the miracle of God's promises. The obstacles may be big, but our God is bigger. The obstacles may be many, but God has an army powerful enough to overcome every single one of them.

The Bible relates the account of an incident when Elisha's servant became extremely fearful when he noticed they were surrounded by great enemy armies. Elisha, on the other hand, was not afraid at all. Why? Elisha's faith eyes were able to see the army of God protecting them, which was much more numerous and powerful than the enemy armies. To help his protégé, Elisha asked God to open the eyes of his young servant so he could also see what really was not visible by the physical eyes.[42] As we look to enter into rest, we too must allow God to open our eyes to His power to handle the obstacles that seem to be blocking us.

Setbacks and Detours

When we've made the decision to pursue the promises of God, we will always face not only obstacles, but there will also be setbacks. Sometimes the setbacks

---

[42] 2 Kings 6:17-20

and detours may not even be your own doing. This was the case with Caleb and Joshua. While they had wanted to obey God and believe in His promise, the rest of the camp did not. So, guess what? They were sent, together with the rest who did not believe and obey God, to the desert for forty years. Similarly, if you have decided to believe that God will bring you to a place of complete rest in your finances, and you started to walk in that faith in giving and tithing. You may face some surprises that would discourage you to go further. The surprises could be things like a leaky basement, accidents, or even losing your job. Instead of seeing increase, all you see is money getting drained from your bank account. The good news is whatever setback you may be facing, what God has promised you, He will surely bring to pass!

There is a sister from our church who experienced something very similar. This sister had been believing for a big promotion in her career for many years. For a while it seemed as though God had forgotten about her. She would interview for the job promotion and it would seem very promising, but in the end someone else would be chosen over her. In fact, at times, she felt like her boss would intentionally prevent her from getting her promotion. There were setbacks, there were lots of disappointments, and lots of betrayals. Yet she continued to trust God and remained faithful in her tithing and giving. A couple of years later, she got hired at another organization that gave her a big promotion in terms of responsibilities and income. You see, a promise is a promise, is a promise, is a promise. If God said it, He will do it. So, if He said you'll have rest, you'll have rest. Whatever promise is given to you, if He said it, you will have it.

Some of you may be contending for Healing. You want to have some rest in your physical body. You've had ailments. You've been struggling and contending. And you're wondering, "Oh God, are You ever going to give me rest from my sickness and rest from my pain?" Friends, may I remind you that if He said it (and He has as far as healing is concerned), then He's going to fulfill it.

Chapter 14

Leave No Man Behind

Read Numbers 32:1-22

Right at the gate of the Promised Land, the tribes of Reuben, Manasseh, and Gad came to Moses and said, "We want to have our possession (our promise) on this side of the Jordan River." This made Moses mad. The reason he was mad was because Moses thought they just wanted to settle and have their rest, and then let their brothers fight their own wars on the other side of the Jordan River. Moses thought they were being selfish.

127

Moses reminded the tribes of Reuben, Manasseh, and Gad of how their forefathers didn't want to go over the River of Jordan to fight either. He reminded them that their ancestors had discouraged the entire congregation of Israel to disobey God; consequently, God promised that they would never enter into the Promised Land and enter into their rest. And if these younger generation was to continue on the same path as their ancestors, the wrath of God would also come upon them. But they explained to Moses that this was not their intention at all. They just thought since the land was good here on this side of Jordan, they were just going to leave their children and their livestock behind. But had fully intended to fight with their brothers until they all had come to their place of rest, the Promise.

This is the principle: We as people of God who have discovered rest and are enjoying that rest, should never ignore or forget those who have yet to find rest. It is never the intention of God for you to be rested alone. If we've discovered rest, you and I need to make sure that others will also discover the rest you are enjoying. For example, if we know someone who is struggling in the areas of condemnation and guilt, struggling in the area of not being able to forgive others, struggling in the area of finances, etc., instead of ignoring their plights and struggles (or worse, making them feel worse by judging or condemning them), we ought to be the mouth and lips of Jesus to bring the good news of rest to them. They need to hear that it is possible to receive rest from their guilt, rest from their struggles, and rest in the presence of God.

Our Churches and Pastors Need Rest

Speaking of leaving no man behind, it is my deep desire to see churches experience true rest. Churches, unfortunately, are some of the most intense places in the world. As a pastor, I can tell you that many of us are striving hard also. Sometimes, I think we pastors are more intense than many other people in the world. Pastors are always looking for more people, more programs, better buildings, better equipment, better performance, etc. And with the advent of social media, things are getting worse. We are constantly being updated about the success of some pastor somewhere in the world. Their successes always make us feel like we need to do more to keep up.

The other day, I saw that one of my pastor friends in California shared with the world pictures of the brand new building for his church that sits five-thousand people. The building is beautiful. I tell you, if I didn't know how to rest, I'd get into the spirit of contention and say, "Well, we're going to do that too! Let's raise some money. Let's buy some equipment. Let's get this rock and roll going. Let's get this show going. If they can do it, so can we!"

Even as a pastor, I want to tell you that it is so easy to get out of rest, especially when we try to compare ourselves with others. When the pastor is out of rest, the congregation will feel it. Some of you have come from churches in which the people were pressured a lot. The congregation was pressured to give, pressured to work, and pressured to sacrifice. Now, I am not knocking giving and serving. It is natural for those of us who have been touched by God to give and serve; however, being pressured to give and serve is another thing. The people are no longer giving and serving out of the place of rest, but from the place of guilt, fear, and condemnation. That's why people are reading this book, because they're running away from those places of restlessness and striving, so that they can come into a place of rest.

If I were ambitious and want to have a big building, then I would be talking to my congregation about money all the time. But thank God we're "contending" to stay at that place of rest. I am contending to stay in that place of rest. I cannot remember the last time I went to my congregation to share the needs of the church. I believe the teaching of giving should be outside the needs of our church. Most importantly, I desire to see that the folks in my congregation to "manifest" that rest in their community, family and amongst their friends. I believe those of us who have discovered true Biblical rest need to be agents of rest! Wherever we are, whoever we meet, we need to be that agent of rest and peace that help bring more stressful soul to the place of rest. By the time people are done interacting with us, they ought to walk away feeling peaceful and feeling at rest.

Chapter 15

Conclusion

Read Joshua 23

According to Joshua 23:1, the children of Israel had conquered all the land/territories that the LORD had promised them. As a result of these victories, Joshua proclaimed, "...the Lord had given rest to Israel from all their surrounding enemies." Now you would think that this would be the end of the story, right? Good ending, right? But that isn't the case because of what happens in the book of Judges, which directly follows the book of Joshua. From the period of the Judges to the time when

Israel was sent into exile (with the exception of when King David and King Solomon ruled), Israel would continue to experience restlessness due to the harassment from their neighbors. These neighboring nations were relentless in pillaging them, harassing them, attacking them, and robbing them of their crops.

Why did this occur? Well, Judges 2 gives us an explanation:

> *10 And all that generation also were gathered to their fathers. And there arose another generation after them who <u>did not know the Lord or the work that he had done for Israel.</u> 11 And the people of Israel did what was evil in the sight of the Lord and served the Baals. 12 <u>And they abandoned the Lord</u>, the God of their fathers, who had brought them out of the land of Egypt. They went after other gods, from among the gods of the peoples who were around them, and bowed down to them. And they provoked the Lord to anger.*

> Judges 2:10-12 (ESV)

Here we learn that this new generation did not know about God and His miraculous works. Consequently, they forsook God and abandoned His presence, which in turn got them out of rest. And as I said, this is not only true for the generation after Joshua but throughout the history of Israel. Every time when they turned away from God, hardship and struggles would follow. However, every time when they turned their hearts towards God and worshipped Him again, rest would ensue.

Centered Around God

Friends, true rest is only possible in the presence of God. God must be the center of our rest. If you want to have rest in all areas of your life, you need to have God be at the center of your rest. If God is not the center of your rest, you'll find your rest depletes very quickly. The enemy will come and look for weak/vulnerable points to yank you out of rest. Every time the people of Israel forgot about God, or every time when they turned away from Him, the attacks from their enemies would soon follow. For many years as a pastor, I have witnessed many sincere believers discover their rest in God. Yet after a while, they started to get attracted to the things of the world and turned their attention away from the Lord. Soon they would stop coming to church, never mind about worshipping the Lord and focusing on Him daily. Paul the Apostle said that "it is through this craving that some have wandered away from the faith and pierced themselves with many pangs."[43]

Do not misinterpret me for preaching fear. I'm not saying God is going to be mad at you and send wrath on you. He doesn't do that. He loves you. But unless you are preoccupied with Him, the devil will occupy you with something else. Unless you are preoccupied with God and His glory, the devil will occupy you with something else, which usually comes with lots of strife and pain[44].

---

[43] 1 Timothy 6:10b
[44] Matthew 12:44-45

In my experience, new believers usually encounter incredible rest when they become born again. For a while, they would fall in love with Jesus, and become super happy. Nothing in the world would matter to them. It's like they got rest on all sides. They could be dead broke yet they have not a care in the world. Then, after a few months or a year, the cares of this world would start to creep into their mind. They would soon lose their focus and attention on God. They would then allow themselves to get worried about different things. Before you know it, they completely lose their rest and become all stressed out like the rest of the world.   Friends, our rest must always center around the glory of God. If you find yourself out of rest, renew your heart and start focusing on God again. As you do, you will soon get that rest back.

For His Glory

"You know that David my father could not build a house for the name of the Lord his God because of the warfare with which his enemies surrounded him, until the Lord put them under the soles of his feet. But now the Lord my God has

given me rest on every side, there is neither adversary nor misfortune. And so, I intend to build a house for the name of the Lord my God, as the Lord said to David my Father. 'Your son, whom I will set on your throne in your place, shall build the house for my name'"

1 King 5:3-5 (RSV).

From this scripture we just read, we see that the Kingdom of Israel had finally come to a complete rest. King Saul proclaimed that the Lord has given them "rest on every side". Wow, what a place to be!

As you implement what has been suggested in this book, I believe you too will come to that same complete rest. Perhaps, sooner than you realize. You will have rest from your sickness, rest from struggling in your finances, rest in your relationships, rest in whatever area of your life in which you are enslaved. You will not be fighting and striving anymore. All of a sudden you will be able to smell the roses, see the sun rise and enjoy even the snow falling. You will notice all the beauty around you that most people will never be able to see in their lifetime because they're so focused on surviving and fighting. When that happens, what will you do?

Another Trap

Over the years, I have known many brothers and sisters in the Lord that have come to full rest in their lifetime. After coming into that full rest, they now have all the energy and resources at their disposal that they didn't have before. What did they do? They got themselves involved in something "bigger" and got themselves out of rest again. For example, I have seen many believers have their mortgages paid off. Instead of enjoying their rest and doing what Solomon did (I will cover this shortly), they decided to buy a bigger house that they actually didn't need. Now they found themselves with a bigger mortgage. Why? Because the world tells them that they need to have a bigger house, a better car, a bigger this, and a better that.

In the end, they would find themselves with contention and stress in their lives all over again. King Solomon said:

"Better is one handful with tranquility than two handfuls with toils and chasing after the wind"

Proverbs 4:6 (NIV).

Friends, may I suggest a more powerful alternative that will not only bring great benefits and rest to you in this lifetime, but will bring great impact to the many generations to come, even after you've long gone home to be with the Lord? May I suggest you do what Solomon did?

Contend for His Glory

Although Solomon built for himself a bigger home, what propelled him to a place of prominence in history and caused him to make a tremendous mark in the world is that when he had found full rest, he put all his energy into building something for the glory of God. He built the most glorious temple in the history of Israel, in fact, in the history of humanity.

Now, we don't necessarily need to build a temple these days because now God dwells in our hearts, but I would propose that you nevertheless contend for the glory of God. I truly believe that being able to bring glory to God is the very purpose for which God wants us to find rest. If we can contend for His glory, not only will He manifest His glory through us, but we will reap incredible benefits for ourselves and, as I said, for the many generations to come. Yes, we may end up with a bigger house or a bigger car, but the specifics are not what matters. The point is, God will multiply His blessings over our lives as we seek and contend for His glory.

Solomon spared no expense in his days for the glory of God. It was said that there was so much gold dedicated to build the Temple that silver was as common as stones – worthless![45] Friends, if you want your legacy

---

[45] 1 Kings 10:27

to be powerful, if you want to build something great, if you want to make a mark in history, build for the glory of God. Spare no effort and expense for His glory. I tell you, if you focus on God's glory, not only will He bless you in this life, He will cause generations to come to be blessed because you're willing to seek after His glory. Don't focus on building a bigger house; that will come. Focus on building for the Lord. When Solomon focused on building the house of God, glory came to his household, his reign, and the entire country.

It is often said that in Toronto, many of the big mansions are mostly empty because the rich people with big houses are often alone, all by themselves. Perhaps only one or two people live in those huge homes. The truth is, most of those mansions are not built for comfort anymore. They are just status symbols. Friends, often we do things not for functional needs, but for recognition and status. I encourage you not to seek your own recognition or your own status; instead, seek for the glory of God. He will lift you up. He will cause you to make a huge mark.

He will cause you to be recognized. Don't strive for it. Don't contend for it. Build for the glory of God. Let God tell you what He wants you to do. Invest your soul, your heart, and your resources to build for the glory of God, then you will truly come to full rest in perpetuity!

.

More Resources

If this book has blessed you, you may find many free online resources helpful also. Please visit us at www.willowdale.tv for Pastor Paul's other teaching resources.

Visit Us In Toronto

If you are in the Toronto, Ontario, Canada area, please come and be our guest, and enjoy the atmosphere of rest and peace. You will be rejuvenated and strengthened in the presence of God. For more information on our church, please visit us at www.willowdale.com

If you wish to contact us, you can:

Write to us or visit us. Our address is:

Willowdale Community Christian Assembly
172 Drewry Avenue
North York, ON
M2M 1E4

Email us:

rest@willowdale.com

Call us:

Canada & US: Toll Free 1-866-357-5089
Local and oversea: +1-416-850-1252

Follow us:

@willowdalelife

Made in the USA
Middletown, DE
09 November 2019

78307445R00097